On My Own
Decoding the Conspiracy of Silence

A Memoir by
Erika Schulhof Rybeck

Summit Crossroads Press
Columbia, Maryland

Published in the United States by Summit Crossroads Press, Columbia, MD.
E-mail Address: sumcrossroads@aol.com.

Author can be reached at waltrybeck@aol.com

ISBN: 978-0-9834049-9-6

LCCN: 2013952485

Dedication

This story, mostly of my years in Austria and Scotland, is dedicated to

- My heroic parents, Friedrich and Gertrude Schulhof, who saved me from being murdered with them.
- To my mother's sister Ellie who, with her husband Bertie and son Hans, all died at the Terezin concentration camp.
- To my mother's other sister Mia and her husband Fritz Treuer who escaped to America and eventually brought me here to have the long fulfilling life with a wonderful husband and wonderful children that my parents had wished for me.

Searching

We sift through the ashes of our past
Children no more
Yet searching forever
For the lost years
For the lost tears
For the lost faces
For the lost places
Of our lost childhood.

--Erika Rybeck, 1970

Contents

Searching iii

Dedication iii

Introduction v

PART I – Austria 1

Birth 1

Mother and Father 3

Grandmother 12

My Magic Kingdom 15

Vienna—Still Shielded from Reality 31

PART II – Scotland 41

Cocooned in a Convent 41

Cottages, Castles and Country Houses 51

Many Mothers—Sacred Heart Nuns 67

A Famous Relative Appears 71

War in the Eyes of Youngsters 81

War Ends, Boarding School Ends—Then What? 87

PART III - America 93

Unraveling the Conspiracy of Silence 93

America at Last 94

Steep Learning Curve 95

Teacher or Learner? 99

From Dream World to Reality 101

Poignant Letters 105

People Misunderstand 107

The Lucky Ones 110

Answers Half a Century Later 111

My 2011 Tsunami 115

Discovering Ancestors 119

Full Circle 121

Postscript: The Rest of My Life 122

Acknowledgements 125

Introduction

My first years were spent in Austria—1928 to 1939. These years prepared the way for Adolph Hitler to march across Europe, ignite World War II and try to decimate the Jewish people. For me, however, these were the blessed days of an innocent and happy childhood. Kept completely in the dark about the turmoil raging around me, I was given no preparation for or understanding of what happened next.

In May 1939 I found myself on a Kindertransport train heading to a convent boarding school in Scotland. My next ten years in Scotland had no connection to my former life—a different country, different culture, different language, different friends and different teachers. My parents, in their successful attempts to shield me, asked everyone in contact with me to say nothing about the tragic events happening in Europe or the desperate state of affairs of many family members, themselves included.

Totally enveloped in my new country and school life, I forgot my native language. My days were so disconnected from the first phase of my life that at times I even wondered if memories of my early childhood were simply a dream. After graduating from high school and two years of college, my ten Scottish years ended as abruptly as my first ten years in Austria.

America welcomed me to my third life. I joined an aunt and uncle, the only close relatives who escaped to survive the Holocaust. While living with them in Ohio and earning my BS at the University of Dayton, I began to glimpse the tremendous events that had been hidden from me.

As an adult it became clear that the disconnect between my three distinct segments needed to be dealt with, but there never seemed to be time. I had not been able to share my Austrian life with my Scottish friends, nor my Scottish life in a convent school with my American friends. None of my friends knew me in all three phases of my life, so there were none to help me connect the dots. I was on my own. So at age 84 I finally have the time to try to fit together the pieces of my fractured past.

Erika's compelling story of a life lived from childhood through adulthood during the Holocaust years and beyond is an attractive and emotional experience for readers of all ages. Her exciting and intimate account, told with feeling and humorous sidelights, sheds light on how all this was handled by one family—an unforgettable tale.

--Dorothy Raphael, MSW

PART I: Austria

Birth

"The stork brought me." This explanation of how I came into this world sufficed for many years. We often saw storks on people's roofs. The fact that I had never seen one with a baby didn't faze me a bit.

According to my birth certificate, I was born December 30, 1928 in the Rudolfiner House, a private hospital in Vienna, Austria. I was the only child of Friedrich and Gertrude Schulhof. The little village of Hohenau on the Czech border was my home for the first nine years of my life. My parents had a spacious apartment within the grounds of the Hohenauer Zuckerfabrik, the sugar factory which employed most of the locals in the community. My father was manager and chief chemist and I could see with pride that he was looked up to by everyone.

The photos that remain of my early years start with the traditional pose of nude on a bear rug, and then show a well-fed baby.

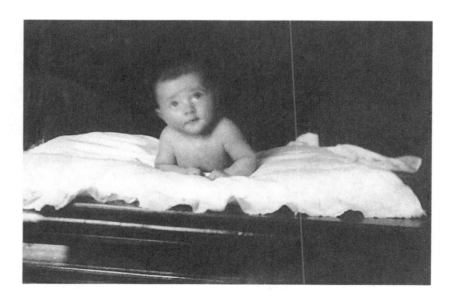

Then there's a girl feeding a baby deer with a bottle. I believe the other fawn was trying to steal a snack from me. It was almost ready to fend for itself. How did I happen to have these pets? In the hunts, described later, a doe might be shot and her fawn brought back to be raised until it could be returned to the woods.

The delivery by stork was an appropriate entry into this fairy-tale compound in a remote fairy-tale village that was my home for the first wonderful years of my life.

Mother and Father

My parents' love sustained me throughout my life, even though I never saw them after I was ten. So it is comforting and helpful for me to look back to those early years—which is a way of thanking them for the great gifts they gave me.

Gertrude Weil Schulhof, known as Trude

Memories of my mother are like looking into a kaleidoscope, little snatches of different scenes. I remember listening to her read the fairy tales of Hans Christian Ander-

sen and, as soon as the story ended, pleading for a repeat performance. My bedtime ritual included first mommy and then daddy kissing me goodnight.

Since social life was limited in our little village, it was very special to see my parents in evening clothes. On one such occasion I recall how beautiful my mother looked in black lace and how cool her pearl necklace felt against my skin as she bent over me for a goodnight kiss. Many years after the war I received a package containing that very dress and a little fur cape, as well as other items my parents had put in storage, presumably hoping that if I got them I might remember those long ago days—which of course I do.

Another picture appears. This time my mother is totally enveloped in a fur coat as she pulls me on a sled to a frozen pond. Many children are there learning to skate. I can still feel the triumph of being able to go in reverse.

My mother was a product of her time. She had no profession or job after she married. However, in retrospect, I feel sure that she worked quite hard managing a household without the many conveniences that we take for granted today. Although we had a maid, there was more than enough for two people to do. We had no car, so anything mother bought from a store would require a half-hour walk to and from the village. Meal planning and some cooking and baking, as well as shopping, were on my mother's agenda. She supervised the laundry and cleaning. And me.

As I learned later, mother was born in Brno, Czechoslovakia in 1895, so she was 33 when I was born. She met my father, a very distant relative, and married him in Prague in March 1928.

Friedrich Schulhof, known as Fritz

My father was a doctor of philosophy and chemistry, but to me he was my hero and I worshipped him. From my point of view, he could do anything. He created

rubies and emeralds in his laboratory and brought them home for me to play with. He told the best stories, he drew pictures and he painted beautiful landscapes, including my very first book when I must have been close to two.

In his youth my father loved to hike in the mountains in the Austrian lake district of Kärnten. After I was married, my husband and I went to the little town of Steindorf on Lake Ossiach and introduced ourselves to the aged owner of the Hotel Post. Amazingly, she clearly remembered my father as a young man, and she took out dusty albums of old guest books to show me the very times he stayed there. She recalled that he would arrive after hiking down the mountain behind town with his rucksack on his back and singing as he approached the hotel.

There was no toy store in our village, so my dad made me a train set and the landscape with mountains and a lake to go with it. He often wrote poems, not just for me but for any occasion that offered itself. He also loved to draw—even making me a little book of things I loved to look at, eat or play with, like the examples of my monkey and a porcelain duck, that I must have called "Aff" and "Pa-pa-pa-pa-pa."

My father was born in 1885 in Krakow, Poland, then part of the Austrian-Hungarian Empire. His father, a surgeon in the army, was stationed there at the time.

He earned his doctorate degree in chemistry at the University of Vienna in 1906. He became chief chemist and manager of the Hohenau Sugar Factory which was owned by his cousins, the Strakosch brothers. He was recognized both as an expert in

Aff and Pa-pa-pa-pa-pa as painted by my father.

Big Father, Little Me

sugar beets and in the industrial machinery and processes used to extract the sugar. His articles about his findings in these matters appeared in professional journals.

When World War I erupted in Europe, my father served as an officer in the Austrian army. He made sketches of battlefield scenes and kept a journal revealing the absurdity of commanders who kept moving their troops back and forth with no apparent strategy, losing more men each time they reversed positions. He himself was eventually captured and spent time as a prisoner of war in Italy.

He resumed his work at the Hohenau Sugar Factory, married

Villa Habig, Hohenau

my mother when he was 42, and continued in his profession until he was forced out and had to flee the town because of his Jewish heritage when the Nazis took over Austria in 1938.

My Parents Seen Through the Eyes of Trautl and Edith

To help paint a portrait of my parents, I jump ahead from the 1930s to 1994. I had taken my husband to Austria to show him the village where I grew up. Very unexpected events brought me back in touch with the family of my childhood years.

We drove to Hohenau from Vienna with Lisa Gassauer, a distant cousin who had returned to Vienna from Switzerland at war's end, and whose husband had regained ownership of the sugar factory that had been in our family for 125 years. After lunch at Villa Habig, their country house in the factory compound, Lisa said I would meet a lady who remembered my parents.

As we sat on the patio, the crunch of gravel announced the arrival of a white-haired lady pedaling up the path on a bicycle and clutching a big bunch of roses. She handed the bouquet to Lisa and, shaking my hand warmly, said: "Do you remember me? My name is Trautl."

With some discomfort I confessed that I did not. It turned out that she was ten years older than I, not a playmate but practically an adult in my eyes half a century earlier. Wiltraut "Trautl" Kobsik quickly said she understood.

"You look like your father," She said. "What a wonderful man he was. My father was also in management and we lived in the same multi-family house as you and your parents. That house was just about 100 yards from here. It was burned down by the Nazis as they fled from the advancing Russian army."

"What can you tell me about my parents?" I prodded.

"Everybody loved them," she assured me. Her detailed memories were astonishing. She told how every fall, at the beginning of the "campaign" when the factory went into high gear for three months to turn the newly harvested sugar beets into the finished product, there would be a gathering of the factory personnel. She said my father would introduce every member of the management team with a poem, gently poking fun—an annual event that was eagerly anticipated by all concerned.

Trautl then told me an almost unbelievable story. A friend of hers was vacationing in Villach in the south of Austria. She sat on a bench next to a stranger who asked where she was from. "A place nobody heard of, called Hohenau," her friend replied.

Excited, almost agitated, the stranger replied, "I know Hohenau very well. I spent many summers there at the home of the Schulhofs." She introduced herself as Edith Weinberger from Vienna.

Apparently word had gotten around Hohenau that Erika Schulhof Rybeck might be visiting Hohenau from America shortly. When Trautl's friend mentioned that to Edith, she became even more excited and begged her to give her phone number to Erika. So Trautl now had that number and urged me to phone when I returned to Vienna.

On the way back to Vienna I tried to recall who this person might be. Her last name meant nothing to me. But then I did recall an Edith and a poem. As a child I had a book in which my friends would write a few lines to remember them by. In my mind's eye I now visualized a little picture of a girl called Edith pasted under a poem she had written about me.

**MY LITTLE FRIEND-
WROTE:**

*I dearly love
Two little doves on the roof,
But I love you, dear Erika,
Even more.*

> *From your friend
> Edith*

With trembling hands I picked up the phone and listened as Edith—yes, the Edith in my autograph book—wept and told me how she had been trying to find me for the past fifty years. Then she told her remarkable story, revealing between sobs what kind of person my mother was.

Edith was the youngest child of a poor family in Vienna that could not even afford the basic necessities. She came into my life because Hohenau, like other small villages, gave poor children plenty of fresh air and good food in exchange for their being helpers for the families that took them in. Here, in her words, is Edith's story of her first arrival in Hohenau:

In 1931 I came with a train full of children to Hohenau and was supposed to find a home. The children were all between 11 and 16 years old. Except for me. I was only a little more than five, and small for my age as well. I was not supposed to go on this trip. Rather, my 12 year old sister was scheduled to go, but she became sick at the last moment and my mother put me on the train in her place.

When we arrived in Hohenau, the townspeople quickly picked all of the older girls and became their host families. Nobody chose me.

So I stood at the railroad station in Hohenau in tears, feeling very alone. Fortunately your mother was walking by the station holding your hand. "Mutti" took me in her arms and comforted me with the words, "O come along little one, don't cry. I'm now your foster-mutti, and this is my daughter Erika, your new sister who will love you very much."

In the evening we were both of us at supper when Papa came home, and I still have his words in my ear. "Oh, when did we get a second daughter?" He took both of us lovingly, one under each arm, and put us to bed. That was my first day in your family circle.

And that is how I began the happiest period in my life. I was allowed to enjoy many wonderful happy times in Hohenau with the Schulhofs –during yearly school holidays and often at Easter time and Pentecost holidays as well.

At times I met your grandmother there too. She used a living place in your house on the ground floor, so I didn't realize her actual resi-

dence was in Vienna. Your parents did so much for me. My visits with you suddenly stopped in 1937.

Edith recalled further that the first thing my mother did was to send for a dressmaker to have a complete outfit made for her. She said I let her play with all my toys. Of course, as an only child of three, I was thrilled to have a playmate. I had always supposed my parents simply brought Edith into our household as my companion, not realizing she had been "rescued," as it were. At any event, after that first summer, they took the initiative of bringing her back again and again.

As we continued talking, I could hardly believe that, after such a long time—over half a century—Edith could describe every detail of my room and our apartment. Her greatest regret, she said, was that she never had the opportunity to tell my parents that she loved them every bit as much as her own. She had kept a postcard from my mother, inviting her for a last visit to Hohenau, and promised to send me a copy—which she did.

I never knew until this conversation that my mother and Edith's mother had kept in frequent touch and that my mother had sent "care packages" to Edith's family for years.

Edith said she and her mother were not notified about what happened to us after we left Hohenau. She did not know that I was sent on a Kindertransport to Scotland or that my parents, after a few years in a kind of Jewish ghetto in Vienna, were shipped to Poland to be murdered. I can only guess that my parents did not write Edith's Catholic family about our fate for fear such a letter would put them under suspicion or worse. When the war ended, Edith said she started an unsuccessful search for us. She was amazed, as was I, that we finally made contact.

I was deeply touched when Edith told me that the times she spent with my family were "the golden years" of her life. I hung up the phone filled with more emotions than I can express. I had been granted a revelation that gave me comfort about my dear parents.

My Parents Remembered

The words of Trautl and Edith comforted me and inspired me to write the following words about my very special mother and father:

The righteous are honored not by tombstone inscriptions but in hearts engraved with priceless memories of good deeds and kindnesses never forgotten.

Grandmother

"Hoch geboren gnädige frau"—which means literally "highly born gracious lady," a class distinction when such distinctions were not politically incorrect in Europe—was the way letters to my grandmother were addressed in her day, back in the early 1900s.

Helene Goldschmidt Schulhof was the wife of Anton Schulhof, a regimental surgeon in the Kaiser's army of the Austro-Hungarian Empire. He was stationed in Krakow, now in Poland, but then part of the empire. They had two sons, my father and my

Uncle Hans. When the sons were young, Anton committed suicide, apparently because he had contracted a highly contagious disease from soldiers he had treated and that he knew was incurable. My grandmother therefore was widowed at a very young age.

I knew her as Oma, and in her eyes I could do no wrong. As she wrote in my little memory book: "Whether you are well behaved or naughty, I love you." No wonder I loved her with fierce devotion.

I have documentation about Oma's distinguished husband, grandfather Schulhof. As an adult, I came to possess many family papers. Among them is this early commendation he received from Emperor Franz Joseph after the battle of

Königgrätz, in which the Prussians badly defeated the Austrians. Anton was only 21 and a student surgeon when he received the following letter:

His Imperial Royal Apostolic Majesty

In recognition of service in the last exercise with great loyalty and fidelity in your dedicated support of the mission by the government as well as the special missions in reference to the taking care of the wounded and sick members of the regiment. He supported and nursed them. Expression of the highest satisfaction in the impeccable form in which he performed all the tasks assigned to him. It therefore serves our great pleasure to express our deeply felt appreciation of his services and convey this to your attention.

Vienna, December 11, 1866
To the signally outstanding
student surgeon, Anton Schulhof

I did not know Oma well since she lived in Vienna while our little family lived in Hohenau, which was a major train trip away in those days. Several times a year she would come for a visit and at other times my mother and I spent time with her in her apartment.

I remember being impressed by the busts of composers and other famous people sitting on top of her bookcases. My favorite piece of furniture in her apartment had many narrow drawers. Each drawer contained a glorious display of the world's most exotic butterflies mounted under a glass cover—specimens collected over the years by my father but always kept at his mother's.

My mother's parents both died when she was a little girl, so Oma was the only grandparent I ever knew. However, I didn't know what I was missing and Oma's love was more than enough for me. I thought that one very special grandmother is what everyone else had. She was small and somewhat bent over but she filled the shoes of all the fairy godmothers and other special beings I could imagine.

As I will relate in the tale of my Vienna year, the ending of her life was very sad.

Grandma Schulhof, my Oma

My Magic Kingdom

I relish revisiting my early years with my parents where God was in his heaven and all was right with the world.

My world from 1928 to 1938 was the village of Hohenau where the March and Thaya rivers come together. We were on one side of the River March; if we crossed the little bridge we would be in Czechoslovakia. My happiest and most intense childhood memories are from this period.

Our part of Austria was very flat, as was the farmland part across the border. However, Czech mountains, the Carpathians, seemed to pop up on the horizon on clear days.

The Sugar Factory

Hohenau's claim to fame was the Hohenau Sugar Factory that employed a large number of the villagers. The factory belonged to the Strakosch family. My father was a cousin of the owner and as Herr Director managed the enterprise and headed the chemical lab. We lived within the Sugar Factory compound that was adjacent to the

Town hall and clock tower in tiny Hohenau village.

Hohenau Sugar Factory, From a painting by Manni Von Werther, nee Strakosch, noted artist and cousin of my father's.

village, but somewhat apart from it. It was the only industry and the major employer of Hohenau workers.

What a fantasy for a child! Trains came through as did carts pulled by oxen. Smokestacks, warehouses and buildings filled with machines and laboratories filled the industrial sections.

The chemical lab was the domain of my father, Herr Director. He was a chemical engineer as well as manager of the enterprise. Since my father always came home for our main meal at noon, it never occurred to me as a child that he really "worked."

To me the factory compound was a fantasy world. Engineers sometimes gave us children rides on their locomotives. In a warehouse of the factory itself I would climb up mountains of sacks of sugar—sitting at the top and listening to an oom-pa band made up of factory worker musicians.

Among the many other buildings in the compound were stables filled with horses, carriages and sleighs because few Hohenau families owned cars in the 1930s.

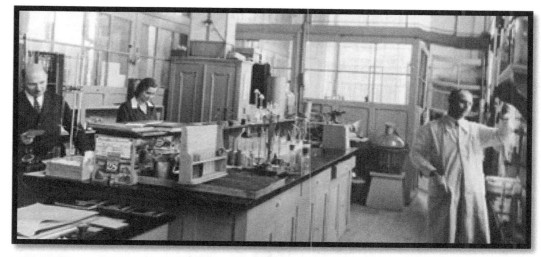

The factory owners, the Strakosch family, resided in a large mansion; that is, when they were not in Vienna or travelling, which was often the case. Since my father was a relative, my parents occasionally were invited to the mansion for the evening. I still remember the excitement in our home before those affairs. Looking back, these events must have been so special because of the near absence of social life for adults in our tiny town.

Across a large courtyard from the mansion house was the building where I lived with my parents. A lilac hedge was on one side and a park with grass and trees on the other. Our apartment on the second floor consisted of a sun room, a living-dining room, my parents' bedroom, my bedroom, the bathroom, a large kitchen and a pantry. Still another bedroom downstairs was for our live-in maid. Other apartments in the building were occupied by other management families. Surrounding most of our apartment was a wide balcony with a most unusual feature—a hole in the flooring through which came the trunk of a huge tree. This stood at the door that led into our apartment.

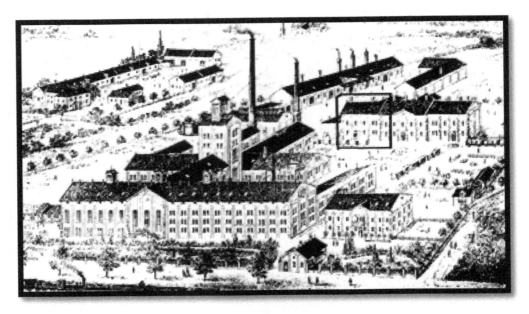

An 1868 engraving of the Factory Compound. Drawn lines mark our residence...square structure, bottom right, is Strakosch mansion.

The Garden

Best of all for me were many happy hours spent in the garden. Growing up, it was a large part of my universe. Magically, things were always changing and yet there was a rhythm to these events that created an atmosphere of order and security. To this day, I can see my garden in my mind—more clearly than what I see in a photo of a two-and-a-half-year-old naked child among the blossoms, or another, taken several years later, with my watering can.

I remember where the flower beds were located, where the trees stood, and where the hedge ran along the path down the center.

I know exactly where the yellow and red raspberries stood at attention—they guarded the left border. I visualize where the blackberries reigned supreme along the back border. The special flavor of their warm ripe fruit is etched in my memory because of treats on special occasions: Wicker laundry baskets were filled with those berries that had survived the frequent attacks by me and my friends, or with cherries and strawberries if they were in season. After much cranking of handles, these fruits of the garden became the most glorious ice cream.

The tulip bed was my father's pride. The scent of the fully opened blooms was in-

toxicating. Although the riot of colors in shades of pink, red, and yellow were astonishing, my father also had a strange determination to create a totally black tulip. Looking back, I suppose that he hand-pollinated various blooms to form different new bulbs, but I don't believe he ever quite succeeded in producing a black tulip.

Harvesting with cook.

My favorite tree was a large walnut, not so good for climbing but generous with the nuts we loved to gather.

The rain barrel was a spot for water play and for the fun of finding a friendly

Me and my bear.

On my way to the sandbox

hedgehog nestled in its base. A few steps away was a rock garden where I watched green and blue lizards dart between the stones.

Since I had no interest in vegetables, I don't recall where they were planted. The hedge however loomed important for a peculiar sport. In summer round white berries appeared. My friends and I delighted in picking them, tossing them onto the paved path and finally stomping on them. Our reward was a rat-a-tat-tat of loud pops as each berry was crushed.

Behind the hedge stood a little shed where garden tools were kept. We seldom went there because it was in the shade and had no windows. Although it was kind of spooky, we overcame our fears during games of hide and seek.

Between the rain barrel and the rock garden was a sand pile. Hours of happy play with pail and shovel resulted in mountains and rivers, even castles. When I daydream I can still feel the sun on my back, the breeze on my forehead and the sense of total peace—a feeling that this was my world and I belonged in it.

Dress Up and Grown-Ups

One of my favorite pastimes was dressing up in my mother's elegant slips that were decorated with fake flowers. I also had an authentic Czech folk costume, from the region of my mother's childhood, shown in the next photo. Another picture shows me in

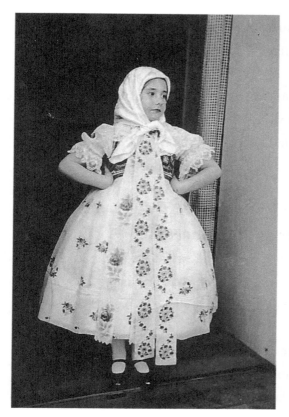 

my Little Red Riding Hood dress.

My father's brother, Uncle Hans Schulhof, and his wife Aunt Thes made a yearly pilgrimage from Vienna to visit us. They would rent a place in the village and Uncle Hans, who was a banker, would help with the financial end of the factory's operation.

I looked forward to this because my aunt and uncle seemed worldly, even exotic in my eyes. They had travelled a lot and enchanted me with stories of faraway places. I cannot forget the thrill of having my aunt share olives which she had brought from Italy. She was also the only person I knew up to that time who used nail polish, and to my delight she occasionally tried a color on my nails.

Autumn—the Hunt and the Campaign

Every fall the forests around the village of Hohenau resounded with gunfire. Oskar Strakosch, the factory owner, would invite guests to join him in the annual hunt.

Of course I did not join them, but I saw the aftermath. It made me feel so sad to see the bodies of rabbits, deer, pheasant and grouse that were brought back. They were on display, hung on trestles in the courtyard to cure. The deer antlers would be mounted and added to a collection in a cottage that was already overflowing with such trophies.

Soon after the hunt came the busiest time of the year in Hohenau. It was called the campaign. That was when the sugar beets were harvested, mostly I believe on farms in Czechoslovakia. The beets would be piled high in carts drawn by oxen that paraded into the compound. Suddenly the factory that had been fairly dormant went into high gear to process the beets.

Joys and Wonder at Christmastime

December was my favorite month of the year. The feast of St. Nicholas, celebrated on December sixth started this special season. Children were alternately happily excited or anxious. As was the custom, I would place my shoes between the double windows of the living room at night.

In the morning I hurried to inspect the shoes in the window. If I had been a good girl, they would be filled with candy and small trinkets. If not, there might be a lump of coal. Next came a visit from St. Nicholas dressed in his white bishop's robe and his

sidekick, Krampus—the devil!—with switches and chains. Instead of Ho Ho Ho, St. Nicholas would remind me to be good and kind while Krampus, a frightening spectacle dressed in black and red, rattled his chains.

Store windows in the village were filled with candies and cookies, many in the shape of St. Nicholas or Krampus, wrapped in shiny black and red cellophane. Little furry devils adorned the packages, and these often wound up in the lapels of villagers' coats and suits. The feast day was a time for merriment and the beginning of the countdown to Christmas that was so eagerly awaited by every child.

Strangely enough my memories of those Christmases had little to do with toys. The preparations and anticipation were a big part of what made the holiday special.

As Christmas approached there was much activity in the kitchen. Lebkuchen and other long-keeping cookies were baked in large batches and stored on pantry shelves. The smells, remembered to this day, were intoxicating. The apartment was filled with the scent of cloves, cumin and other spices. Ginger cookies, vanilla kipferl and linzer tortes appeared.

Another yearly ritual was the trip to the village to select a carp, swimming around in a barrel. Wrapped in a damp towel, the poor creature was brought home and set free in the bath tub until a blow to the head set it free from this world and it made its appearance at supper the night before Christmas.

On Christmas Eve my parents got rid of me by shipping me off to Uncle Hans and Aunt Thes at their place in the village. During my absence my parents had time to put up a tree and surround it with gifts. The idea was to surprise me and it always worked, year after year.

As evening approached it was time for uncle and auntie to take me home. We would crunch through the snow for perhaps half an hour until we arrived. I would approach home with great anticipation. The living room door would be closed and magic was in the air. With my eagerness to see what was in there, it seemed to take forever to get out of my boots and all the clothes I had been bundled up with.

Suddenly the tinkle of a bell announced the moment I had seemingly waited for all year. The door opened and there in all its splendor was the Christmas tree. With beating heart I would drink in the scene before me. The flames of real candles flickered. Sparklers, hanging down like icicles, sent showers of sparks in all directions.

Unlike today when piles of gifts are arrayed in fancy boxes, my presents were few and displayed unwrapped beneath the tree. Often they were books. Once there was a teddy bear as big as me. Instead of buying them, my father made toys for me. The most memorable was a little train set he carved from wood, and he made a landscape with mountains and a lake for the train to go round.

I would admire the tree and the gift but was not allowed to touch anything until I had performed for the assembled adults a poem or song prepared for the occasion. At that moment I had no doubt that my parents were the most wonderful people in the world and that the world was the most wonderful place imaginable.

After a dinner of carp, it was almost midnight. On the stroke of twelve a trumpeter stationed in one of the sugar factory towers would blow his horn announcing that Christmas day had arrived.

There was no religious aspect to our Christmas in my family, though I vaguely remember our maid taking me to a church service once in a while.

Another magical part of the winter season was when my parents would bundle me up in sacks of fur and take me for rides in a horse-drawn sleigh. We would race through the snow with bells jingling. Also great fun was ice skating with my mother or my friend Erika Schweinberger, who lived nearby.

Summer Delights

Summer holidays had their own set of rituals. At times a horse and carriage arrived from the stable and we had lovely outings. We would drive clippety-clop into the woods and meadows filled with wild flowers.

Each summer we spent a month or so in the southernmost Austrian province of Kärnten, anglicized as Carinthia. This involved much planning and even more packing.

We went there by train. Mother and I would stay the full time and my father would join us for part of the time.

We stayed at resorts along picturesque lakes—Ossiachersee, Faakersee, Werthersee—nestled among forested mountains. Our days focused around swimming, boating and hiking.

We so much enjoyed nature as a family. My father loved to sketch and soon I was enticed to do the same. For that reason just the sight of a box of colored pencils still gives me a thrill. Sometimes we would rent a boat and row to a village on the opposite shore.   Some of the happiest outings were those when we came across wild strawberries to eat or carry back with us, or when we would find the elusive edelweiss, a white alpine flower with petals that formed stars. Whenever I smell pine it takes me back to the special pungent smell of the evergreen forests we tramped through in beautiful unspoiled Kärnten.

Maybe being an only child led me to concoct odd activities and adopt some strange

Vacation Times in Kärnten, Austria's Lake Country

creatures for companionship. One summer we went to a Yugoslavian island instead of Kärnten and there were lots of snails with large shells. I collected a dozen or so and played school with them. I felt certain that I had trained them and that they "marched" up a tree trunk in orderly fashion because of my instructions. Butterflies were everywhere and they enticed me to catch and mount them. I also created flowers entirely unknown to nature by combining the different stalks and blossoms of the various wildflowers I picked.

One less than blissful episode remains in my memory. Somehow I got a splinter in my finger and it wouldn't come out. My mother went in search of tweezers. For reasons I can't remember I was in dread of that instrument. So I decided to run away, and I did. Before I had gotten very far I felt tired and sat down on a nifty little hillock beside the path. Unfortunately, the ants whose domicile I had unknowingly invaded went into action. Soon I was hopping about and screaming in terror. Thus was my hiding place discovered and I was ignominiously but rather thankfully rescued.

Off to School

The picture of my first grade class shows me as a solemn-faced child. We were stiffly posed in those days when shutter speeds were slow and photographers, instead of telling a group to smile, would warn all of us not to move.

When I think of my first school days, it is the close-knit friendships I remember most. Three of us in my class were called Erika. It happened that all of us Erikas were good students and we worked hard for perfect grades. Sometimes in play my friends would chant, "Erika, Erika, geh zu Amerika." Little did I suspect how prophetic that childish rhyme—"Erika, Erika, go to America"—would turn out to be.

We loved gymnastics and my parents had a teacher come to our house for private lessons for me and my friends. We looked forward to those classes and had lots of fun. Piano lessons also started about this time. I hated them. All I was permitted to do were scales and finger exercises.

I wanted to be a dancer or a movie star. Shirley Temple was my idol and I wrote her a letter of admiration. To this day I have the little book she sent me with pictures of herself in different movie roles.

Jumping ahead many decades… As I mentioned in the chapter about my parents, I took my husband to Hohenau in 1994 to show him the village where I had lived as a child. We saw the sugar factory where my father was manager and chief chemist, the church, my school, and some of the homes in the village, outside of the factory compound. Our own residence was among the many that were either bombed or burned during the war.

Teacher Hilda Drabek and class. I am fifth from left, front row; Erika Berghöfer, later a prominent Austrian actress, is on my left.

Besides my distant cousin Lisa, who drove us there from Vienna, let me repeat that we met only one other person that I had known in my Hohenau days, Wiltraut "Trautl" Kobsik. She was eight years or so older than I—a big difference for a child, so she must have seemed practically an adult to me.

Trautl recalled that during summer holidays she showed Lisa and me and other friends how to act in little dramatic skits and taught us little dances. She even brought me a photo of one recital on the lawn with us little girls posing a la Isadora Duncan in Greek tunics and with hoops. I must have been around four when the photo was taken. The photo next to it reminds me that I used to love wearing a crown of roses in my hair. Almost a lifetime later, I was looking at my wedding pictures and became aware for the first time that my veil was anchored by a wreath of roses—very much like the one in my childhood picture.

Word of my short half-day return to Hohenau apparently spread rapidly through the town after we left. Among those who got the news was Hilda Drabek, my first grade teacher. When we returned to America, I was surprised to find a letter from her. She sent me that class picture on the previous page.

Hilda wrote that she remembered me and my classmates very well because we were the very first class she taught. She was only 20 and had not even finished training but had been called to step in when the regular teacher was suddenly named burgemeister or mayor of Hohenau.

My teacher said I was a very good student. What was most comforting, Hilda, like Trautl, recalled how exceptional and nice my parents were. Once we made mail contact, Hilda faithfully wrote to me every Christmas with news of her family, the village, and the sugar factory. She kept writing well into her late eighties, usually closing by saying, "This is probably the last time you will hear from me." When I received no card in 2002, I feared she had died. Yet in 2010 we got a Christmas card from her daughter who wrote: "Mother's fine at age 96 and sends regards, but she thought you would not like her handwriting." Still a teacher! But that's another story.

I was in that little school in Hohenau till the age of nine. And then…

Abrupt Departure from Hohenau

1938 was a year of tremendous change in Austria. My magic kingdom was not immune. As if by magic, and not the happiest magic, that first part of my life—my little world in Hohenau—ended abruptly and disappeared. I was about to leave it forever.

My parents told me we were going to live with my grandmother in Vienna because she was ill.

As a nine-year-old, I was self-absorbed and took no notice of world events. If there was tension in my house—and looking back, there undoubtedly must have been—I was unaware of it. In that society and in those times, children were not included in concerns of the adult world, and my parents, for reasons that I now fully comprehend, really pushed that approach to its ultimate limits.

At any rate, I was ecstatic with the thought of going to Vienna to live with my grandmother. I adored my Oma. It never occurred to me then to question the reason for this move that was disrupting the whole pattern of our lives.

Yet, having said that and honestly believing it, a flash of momentary uneasiness struck me, because one scene at our departure from Hohenau remains firmly fixed in my memory. When we came down the stairs from our apartment, my mother turned to look back. My father, in a voice I had never heard before, said, "Yes, Trude, have a good look. This is the last home you'll ever have."

The remark puzzled me. Yet I was soon preoccupied with looking forward to the joy of being with my beloved grandmother.

The child of the magic kingdom did not even find it strange—although it was in fact exceedingly strange—that nobody was at the train station to see us off. Or even stranger, that, as we were leaving to live in a different city, we just got on the train without a single piece of luggage.

Vienna—Still Shielded from Reality

During the year I lived in Vienna, my parents kept me from being aware of the dire nature of our situation. Just as my life in the village was not part of the real world, my stay in Vienna was quarantined from what was happening all around me. My dear parents succeeded in making sure that I would remain a secure and happy child as long as we were together. To this day I don't know how they managed to do this.

The things I was not told are so critical to understanding my story that I will merely list some of them here, saving further discussion of those matters until later. Because my parents chose to protect me, I was not told:

That my family, though thoroughly assimilated and not affiliated with any religious organization, had a long and quite illustrious Jewish history.

That all the changes about to take place in my life were associated with the anti-Semitic obsession of the Nazis, to the extent that, under Hitler's doctrines, my parents and I were considered Jewish.

That the Nazis had taken over Austria and, in taking over the sugar factory, had stripped my father from his position.

That, like almost all Austrians of Jewish background, we were in great peril.

Decades later, quite late in my life, I learned to my surprise that a number of practicing Jews lived in Hohenau during my years there. I learned to my horror that, within a day or so after we departed for Vienna, these Jews were rounded up and sent directly to concentration camps where all but one perished. It thus seems apparent that someone who knew of the round-up plans and who was fond of my parents warned them of what was about to happen. This would help explain why we left in such haste.

As I have said, we walked to the station without luggage. Nobody was there to say goodbye to us. The train came and off we went. All the same, I was innocently looking forward and with much anticipation to this change in our lives.

No Greeting from Grandmother

When we arrived in Vienna at my grandmother's apartment, where was she?

My parents told me she was sick. Actually, she was deathly ill, and I was not allowed to see her. Under the new political regime, she may have been denied access to proper doctors or hospitals. My father slept in her room where he tried to care for her.

Grandmother's apartment was not large. The room where she lived out her last days, off limits to me, had been her living room. The dining room sprouted a day bed for me and another bed for my mother. Our sleeping there was an odd arrangement, but following my practice of accepting whatever my parents presented, I don't recall questioning it. An ornate dining table with inlaid woods of different colors was in the center of the room. A grand piano sat near the wall. The hall leading to the kitchen and bathroom was memorable for its variety of busts of musicians and poets and for a cabinet with many narrow shelves that contained my father's amazing butterfly collection.

Several months after our arrival in Vienna, as I was leaving for lessons, I heard my father answer the phone. For my first time ever, I saw that he was crying. "Don't bother to come now, it's too late," he sobbed as he told his brother Hans that their mother was dead. Because I had not been allowed to see her, by the time she died, I had become accustomed to life without her.

Religion and Little Red Erikahood

Once we settled in, my life took on an air of intrigue, and I loved it. During my year in Vienna, I believed I was living an adventure.

Early on, my parents said we would become Catholics. Just as I did not question my parents about why we went to Vienna, I had no problem when they said the three of us were converting.

Three decades later, I visited Olga Kraft in Vienna. She was a distant relative whose side of the family had been Catholic long enough to escape the Nazi onslaught. She and her husband Franz actually safeguarded some of our family belongings for me until after the war. Aunt Olga told me on that visit, "Your parents converted to save you." If true, their goal was certainly successful. Yet it also seems plausible, based on things my parents wrote, that religion gave them considerable solace during their terrifying ordeals.

Previously, my parents listed their religious preference as *religionslos*, or unaffiliated. I believe my father considered himself a *freidenker*, or free thinker. Both my parents were devoted to ethical behavior, great lovers of nature, proud of their family backgrounds, but before our flight to Vienna they were not practicing followers of any organized religion. I don't really know my grandmother's feelings about religion or whether she was exposed to religious training in her early years. But I can visualize almost everything in her apartment, and I can say with confidence that there were no religious symbols or artifacts of any kind in sight.

Back in Hohenau our maid may have taken me a few times to the local church for a Christmas or Easter service. Although my parents practiced no religion, as I have said, nor gave me any clue of our family's Jewish background, we celebrated Christmas in a secular non-religious way. Also, I recall that once a year, around midsummer, a whole caravan of Hohenau people rode carriages through meadows full of flowers and into the woods where there were wreaths around a kind of altar. I now presume there must have been some important religious significance to this festival, but at the time that aspect made no impression on me.

Now, for the first time in my life I had religious instruction. In Vienna I loved going to churches where the candles, the flowers, the incense and especially the music enchanted me. We went to some of the big churches on Sundays where the music was outstanding.

Soon it was arranged that I was to get private schooling lessons at an Ursuline convent not too far from my grandmother's apartment. Again, there was so much I did not know at the time: Nobody told me that I could not go to a regular school because I was supposedly Jewish, nor could I be sent to a Jewish school—if any were still operating—because I had had no Jewish education or familiarity with its festivals.

Innocent of all that, I went surreptitiously to the convent about half a mile away. As I zigzagged several blocks and under a railroad viaduct to the convent, I carried my books in a basket covered by fruit or vegetables. If anybody stopped me, I was presumably just taking food to the good nuns who, as I later learned, had been forbidden to take in students, even though they had long been a teaching order.

I was introduced to Mater Amalia who was to be my personal instructor. She was a no-nonsense kind of woman, quite strict but with a heart of gold. To me and only one other girl she taught arithmetic and history. She wrote in my autograph book, expressing in beautiful handwriting her philosophy and spiritual sense:

Immer, immer suchest Du,
Nimmer, nimmer find'st Du Ruh;
Keiner, keiner stillt den Schmerz,
Einer, einer schuf Dein Herz;
Schuf's für sich für sich allein,
Nur in ihm kann's ruhig sein.
In lieber Erinnerung wird stets
deiner, liebe Erika, gedenken.

4. XI,1928 Mater Amalia, Ursuline

Which I translate as follows:

One is seeking forever and ever, never finding peace.
No person can quiet your suffering. Only One
created your heart, He who created it created it for
Himself alone. Only in Him can one find peace. In
loving memory, I will think about you, dear Erika.

A Most Ironic Attraction

Coming from the Ursuline convent one day, I was walking back to our apartment when I saw a parade of Hitler Youth in their smart uniforms. They all wore swastika armbands as they marched along with precision. Of course, I knew nothing about them or about the superior race ideas with which they were being indoctrinated. All I knew was what I saw. They were boys of about my age or a little older and I was smitten. I stopped in my tracks and lingered quite a while on the sidewalk to get a good look. I watched with delight as the parade went by.

My parents were worried when I came home late. They were not at all amused when I told them why I had been delayed. They probably sensed my thrill at seeing the marching boys and they gave me strict orders from then on to come directly home after school. No lingering. It was unusual for them to be angry with me. I just took it that they were annoyed I was late. I knew nothing about the Nazis and had no idea of the political implications or any sense of danger, nor did my parents explain any of that to me.

In fact I was so innocent about my own background and about the hate campaigns of the times that I was completely puzzled when somebody called me a "dirty Jew" or something like that. It meant nothing to me.

Echo from Hohenau

In the midst of my Vienna life, I was pleasantly surprised to receive a packet of charming notes from my gymnastic classmates and teacher. Very loving. Two of my friends, to show how much they missed me, sketched themselves with tears dripping down.

The selections below show the teacher's note on the right plus two of the many children's messages.

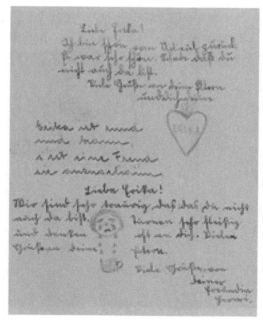 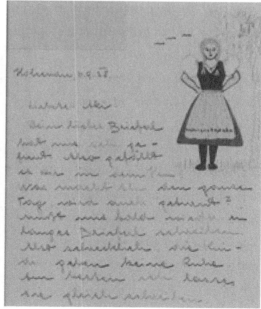

Looking back, I can't help wondering. Did my former playmates have any idea why I left Hohenau suddenly without saying goodbye to them? Like me, were they unaware our family was considered Jewish under the new order? Did the teacher know the Nazis had forced my father out of his job? Was that why, out of concern, that she suggested the girls write to me? Or had the evil ways of the Nazis not yet penetrated the minds of the Hohenau villagers, so that my gymnastic teacher did not realize this little writing exercise might have put her in danger? So many questions. So many answers we'll never know.

Luggage in Advance

Not long after my girlish fascination with the Hitler Youth, my parents promised me a "new adventure," as they put it.

"Guess what?" they said. "We are going to live in America. Uncle Fritz and Aunt Mia have invited us!"

Then they added: "First, however, you will be luggage in advance and go to a wonderful boarding school in Scotland." I had no idea what a boarding school was, but the idea that I would have lots of girls to get to know sounded quite exciting. Being an only child, I had always longed for other children to play with.

I was led to believe that, after a short time in Scotland, my parents would arrive there and then we would all go to America together. There, I assumed, we would "live happily ever after," like in the story books.

At age ten and never having spent a a single day or night away from at least one of my parents, I had no idea what was in store for me. They said I would go on a long trip to a new country where people speak another language. To sweeten the pot, so to speak, I was told that Manschi, a girl my age, would be joining me very shortly after I arrived there.

At the Ursuline convent I met a girl my age called Manschi who, like me, was secretly getting schooling there. Her mother had told her that, like us, they were hoping to live in America. Manschi and I became best friends. Our parents became acquainted. So they planned that we would both be sent to the same boarding school in Aberdeen, Scotland. The thought of having my best friend accompany me on my big adventure obscured the fact that, for the first time in my life, I would be away from my parents and removed from everything familiar.

Wrenching Departure—Kindertransport

I recall a flurry of packing for me. It was mostly clothes, but also a few of my favorite books. As it turned out, I went by myself to Aberdeen because Manschi's visa to Scotland was delayed. She never joined me there. However, she and her mother were lucky enough to escape together to America.

How did I get out of Vienna, since Austria was already occupied by the Germans? The Kindertransport—a children's train—was my means of breaking free. Under a peculiar arrangement, these Kindertransports took refugee children to safety from Germany, Austria and Czechoslovakia. The Nazis apparently were eager, before they developed their killing camps, to get rid of "useless and undesirable" children.

Thanks to Nicholas Winton, an English humanitarian who organized the Kindertransport, the British amazingly opened their doors to ten thousand children, saving most of us from almost certain death. The British did this despite being on the brink of war and already suffering hard times. Especially heroic were the Jewish trainmasters who escorted scores of these trainloads of children through Germany and Holland and across the Channel to England. There, after tasting the breath of freedom, these leaders returned to take more youngsters on more Kindertransport trips. Under terms of the program, if any of the escorts had chosen to stay and escape, the whole Kindertransport enterprise would have been closed down.

Sealed trains carried mostly Jewish children (I was an exception) from Prague, Vienna and Berlin across Germany to Holland, from where they were ferried to England. Most went to families, others like myself to schools or other institutions.

As an adult who clearly recalls what it was like to be the mother of ten-year-olds, I can hardly imagine how my parents managed, when I was ten, to make all the arrangements for me to leave them without instilling in me any doubts or fears. In fact, considering the trauma they were undergoing, I remember with some shame an incident after we left our apartment and were heading for the train station.

We had just walked past a little shop in our neighborhood, and I said, "Wait!" I reminded my mother and father that they had promised me an ice cream cone from that shop before my departure. Although that must have been the last thing on their minds, of course they stopped and let me have my cone.

The Vienna train station was filled with parents and the children scheduled to leave on the transport. It was night time, but the lights in the station helped us find our way to my compartment on the train.

It was eleven at night, Saturday, May 13, 1939, on that fateful day when a whistle blew and a train full of children pulled out of the station. Mine was one of the faces pressed against the window to wave goodbye. I watched the two dearest people in my life waving white handkerchiefs so bravely until they disappeared from view.

It was to be my last glimpse of all that was most precious to me. I never saw them again, but I would not know that until years and years later, hoping against hope that we

Boarding the Kindertransport. From the Harriet and Kenneth Kupferburg Holocaust Resources Center and Archives..

would be re-united.

I often wonder why this journey on the Kindertransport which saved my life and changed it forever is so buried in my memory, when the toy train my father made for me years earlier remains so clearly fixed in my mind. Blotted from my mind is most of the three and a half days en route to my faraway destination. After the rail journey through Austria, Germany and then Holland, we apparently took a ship across the Channel to England. There, in what seemed like a huge hall, I vaguely recall the throng of children gradually disappearing as families or organizations came to pick them up. Someone then must have taken me to the train on which I rode northward by myself for the last day's trip to my destination.

I do clearly remember arriving at the boarding school that was to be my new home for many years. And that is the beginning of the next chapter of my disjointed life.

Mother, Father and I as we were when we saw each other for the last time—and when they made me feel I was simply leaving on a nice adventure

PART II: Scotland

Cocooned in a Convent

May 17, 1939. I have a clear memory of arriving at the beautiful granite mansion at 3 Queen's Cross, the Sacred Heart convent boarding school in Aberdeen.

I was welcomed with a big hug by the school's director when I arrived in the sedate parlor of Queen's Cross. Reverend Mother Mary Paterson then led me down the long main corridor of the school. I was amazed to see the uniformed girls curtsy as she passed. Even more astonishing to me was the fact that the girls all wore white gloves. Inside the school building! Really, Scottish people must be quite peculiar, I thought.

My New Home in Aberdeen—Queen's Cross Convent of the Sacred Heart .

This idea was reinforced the first time I spotted a man wearing a kilt. I was in stitches and immediately wrote my parents that in Scotland men wear pleated skirts.

More surprises followed. Instead of a room, I was shown into a dormitory with cubicles for a bit of privacy.

Top: Aunt Ella Popper. Below: I arrive in Aberdeen, a refugee from Vienna.

Why Aberdeen?

I should pause to explain why, of all places, I happened to arrive at a Catholic boarding school in Scotland. I found out many decades later that my Aunt Ella Popper, on the Catholic side of our family, was prominent in church circles. She had close connections to the Sacred Heart order in Vienna, an order that had highly regarded schools in many countries.

Thanks to Aunt Ella's efforts, my parents learned that the Sacred Heart convent school in Scotland would take me as a "Catholic refugee child," which I was by the time I left Vienna on the Kindertransport. My arrival must have been something of an event because the *Aberdeen Press and Journal* ran this photo of me on May 18, 1939. It shows a perplexed looking ten-year-old. Since I could not understand anybody's English, I probably did not even know why my picture was being taken.

My First English Word

Sister Woods was the first person I got to know in Aberdeen. She was so pretty, with such a rosy face and a sweet smile that I was sure she must be a saint. She made a big impression because I did not yet know anyone else. She taught me my first English word, which was *cardigan*.

As she was helping me get dressed, she had me put on a sweater that was open down the front. "Cardigan," she said, and had me repeat it.

Cardigan is not a word one uses every day. I certainly didn't. But it stuck, thanks to kind and friendly Sister Woods.

Porridge

Then there was the food, most of which was quite unfamiliar. Meals were taken in a refectory of assigned places for six to a table. My dislike for porridge or oatmeal was immediate and permanent. It apparently was cooked the night before, and after we came back from the chapel for breakfast, it had a kind of crust on it with deep crevices. Ugh.

I could not complain because I didn't know the language. Besides, I remembered that my parents had drilled into me that I should always be polite and grateful and make them proud of me. I was totally unprepared for what awaited me. Fitting in at a boarding school was so different than my life at home that I had a hard time finding words to write about it to my anxious parents. I just tried my best to fit in and adjust.

Every Kind of Closet

Compared to what I was used to, the Queen's Cross boarding school was huge. The photo below shows only part of the rear view. Besides its many classrooms and refectory or dining hall, it had a dormitory, corridors that seemed endless, a chapel, a gym, a library, a parlor, a lovely garden, tennis courts and playground. The several buildings and grounds probably took up three acres. The religious community had its private quarters which I never saw because they were off limits to students.

How I got through the first month I don't know. I must have been in a state of shock. I knew no English and no one else that I met, young or old, spoke a word of

Queen's Cross boarding school, rear view.

German. It was total immersion.

Promptly after my arrival I was shown a bathroom, which happened to be upstairs in the large main building. This was a great distance from our classrooms in the adjacent building. Imagine my distress when nature called and the only relief was far away, so that by the time I returned I would be late for my next class.

Needing a facility that was closer, I pleaded, "closet, closet"—with the accent on the last syllable. It was the German word for toilet. No one could figure out what I wanted. They showed me broom closets, coat closets, every imaginable closet except the one I was looking for. This was one of many frustrations that probably motivated me to learn a new language, which I did with amazing rapidity.

Surrogate Mom

Mother MacLennan was in charge of me, and certainly she was part of how I got through my first term at Aberdeen. She was very short of stature, almost a dwarf, with a hump back that was nearly disguised by her habit. She had thick lips and a smile that made me feel loved and cared for. At the very beginning she had to tell me where the classrooms were. She helped me find my way around the place.

Mother MacLennan became a surrogate mom for me. That is, she mothered me in a special way with all the affection of a real mom. During the first few weeks, I spent many nights crying or weeping uncontrollably—possibly a combination of homesickness, experiencing being without my parents for the first time in my life, and not understanding what others were saying or being understood when I wanted to say something. Mother MacLennan would kneel beside me and stroke my hair until I fell asleep.

To the students she taught plain song—Gregorian chant, that is. She was a good dancer and sometimes taught dancing too, as did the gym teacher and Mother MacPherson.

Mother MacLennan kept in touch with me throughout my stay at Queens Cross. According to the rule of the Sacred Heart order that guides the nuns' life and interactions, one was not supposed to get too close to any other human. Rather you were to keep your heart and mind focused on God. In my case, however, as a foreigner who couldn't communicate, Mother MacLennan clearly became closer to me than was usually permitted.

The following story reveals the unusual caring character of Mother MacLennan. Before I left Vienna, Mother received a list of clothes I was to bring to the convent in Aberdeen. Among them was a dressing gown. Since I didn't have one, my Mother knitted one for me out of pretty blue wool. It was fine for several years. But as I grew considerably after the age of ten, it finally became much too small. Knowing the love that had gone into making it, Mother MacLennan painstakingly unraveled it and gave it a new life as a bed jacket that she herself knitted.

There is a bittersweet ending to the story of our relationship, when I was a college student in Edinburgh, as I tell later.

Long-Distance Parenting — Letters from Home

From the moment of my arrival in Aberdeen, I received a constant stream of letters from my mother and father--my Mutti and Papi, each writing to me separately.

They called me Arkelein, Pieperl, Bazala and their other pet names for me. Fortunately I saved those letters and they help tell my story and, to a certain extent, theirs too. So I excerpt, condense and edit brief portions, since most are quite long. I start here with a few lines from the first ones and intersperse other excerpts later.

<u>May 14, 1939.</u>

My dear Arkelein,

I hope you receive this letter when you arrive in Aberdeen. Please write in great detail about your trip and the whole time since our farewell. Your mother is always thinking about you... Many kisses. Your loving Mutti

My Pieperlein,

Yesterday evening you left and today already we are writing to you. On

your journey did you eat the fruit before you crossed the border? How was it in Holland and London? … Much hugging and loving, your Papi.

May 17.

We were happy to receive your 2 cards. Your cut will heal soon. On the trip who braided your pigtails? Will send patent leather shoes and pleated skirt with Manschi. Mutti

You were a good girl to write. Be brave and polite in your new home. I am sure your new mothers and teachers are kind and glad you are with them. Uncle Hans and Aunt Thes are in London already.

Papi

May 18.

Your card from the train arrived.   That your suitcase did not arrive is not good. I will send you Papagei and Kiebitz subscriptions. Kisses. Mutti

Dearest Pieperlein,   Many people send you greetings, Aunt Steffi, and Hohenau head gardener Nowak, whom we met on the street with his wife. Thank dear God that you arrived happily. Can you sleep without your red felt cat? Papi

May 21.

We were delighted to get your letters and even more that everything is turning out well. Write in detail—what time you get up, what you eat for breakfast, what you do every hour of the day. Has the suitcase arrived? Warmest hugs, Mutti

P.S. About our departure, we are no further along. Papa will go next week to Prinz Eugen Strasse to get our passports.

You're so good to be writing. From reading Mother Paterson's letter, we can tell how nice she is to you. Have good manners and be obedient. You are in a lower grade than you were here. As soon as you speak English well

you will be put in a higher grade. You mustn't forget to pray.
Now my dearest Butzlein, many kisses, Papi.

May 25.

The mother of a boy named Peter who was on the train with you sent us a
picture of you that was in an Edinburgh newspaper. I will send the blouse,
stockings, shoes and gloves that you asked for. Manschi has had her medi-
cal exam and will come very soon. We are not any further along in obtain-
ing our travel papers. Write and answer all our questions.
Mutti

You are seeing many new things. How does one play baseball? We sent
stationery and colored pencils. We are so curious to hear you describe a
day in the convent.
Papi

New Dimensions of Religion

Like a sponge I lapped up a new language, new culture, and a new religious life.
My experience in the religious arena to date had been casual. Even in Vienna where I
liked going to mass and hearing fine music with my parents, I knew very little about the
church or a religious life. I sensed that God was someone you prayed to on Sunday or
at bedtime.   To me, Christmas and Easter were chiefly times for presents and fun.

At the convent all that perspective changed. The Sacred Heart nuns were cloistered. Their whole life was dedicated to spirituality and to the education of their pupils.
It was a life of constant striving for perfection through obedience, prayer and self-de-
nial. Saint Madeline Sophie Barat, the founder of the Sacred Heart order, made it her
mission to give students the best education as well as the life style of an aspiring saint.
She laid down the school rule that students were to live by. In reality this rule was a
simpler or slightly watered-down version of the holy rule and discipline followed by the
nuns themselves. It was Spartan and orderly with every waking moment accounted for.
At least in our school in Aberdeen, this rather harsh and strict regimen was modified by
a loving and caring atmosphere.

Our typical day started with a wake-up bell at 6:30 followed by morning prayers and mass. Eight o'clock was breakfast and then an hour of KP duties. Morning classes lasted till noon. After lunch we had a recreation hour which meant field hockey, a walk in a crocodile (as they called a long line of us two-by-two) led by a teacher, or some other outdoor exercise. Then came afternoon classes and tea time. After tea we prayed the rosary and then settled down for homework in the study hall till supper. There was a short recreation period after this and then evening prayers and to bed by nine.

Talking was permitted during meals and recreation only. At all other times we were supposed to read or pray.

Convent life revolved around the liturgy of the church. Every feast day was observed. Some of these holidays were anticipated with great delight. In May we celebrated under the blossoms in the garden. December 8th, the Feast of the Immaculate Conception, was special. Every corner of the building was decorated with shrines and flowers. When it was time for the procession to leave the chapel and wend its ways through the corridors, the lights were lowered and, with candles and lilies in hand, each of us sang our best to honor the Virgin Mary. It seemed like magic and our hearts were filled with wonder and peace.

Judged Before Our Peers

The student body was composed of girls aged 5 to 18. Classes were small, only eight to twelve girls usually. That meant there was a great deal of attention focused on each of us, not only in regard to the subjects we were studying but about our character development and behavior as well.

At the end of each week we girls would face all the nuns in a kind of court. Each girl would be called upon to come forward and receive one of three cards. If your behavior during the week had been acceptable, you would receive a light blue card with VERY GOOD written on it. If you had committed an infraction, such as incomplete homework, talking out of turn, or not paying attention, you might receive a dark blue card with GOOD stamped on it and the reason for it, spoken out loud before the student body. The third card, INDIFFERENT, was yellow and was hardly ever earned by anyone. It meant you had really stepped out of bounds. In this way we were informed of our progress or lack thereof in behavior or demeanor.

One chubby, blue-eyed blond with the appropriate name of Angela never seemed to get a bit of criticism. So I asked her how she could be so good. "It's easier to be good," she said sweetly, and her saying this so sweetly and angelically did not endear her to me.

This judging business became such an expected part of our routine that, years later, I still found myself looking to others to tell me how well—or how poorly—I was doing.

Sheltered Life Away from Parents

Living closely together night and day created intense relationships between girls as well as with teachers. Our lives were totally contained within those granite walls and the real world soon disappeared. In Aberdeen, as in Hohenau and Vienna, I was encapsulated in a kind of bubble that kept me cut off from the momentous events of the times—so much so that others who lived through those same times find it hard to believe how utterly innocent and sheltered I was.

Emotionally, I comforted myself with the understanding that my parents would be coming for me very soon. As can be seen from excerpts of those letters that arrived almost daily, my letters back to them often were less than satisfactory. They kept begging for more precise news of my activities. Now as an adult and a parent it is clear to me how their pain of separation from their only child made them hunger for every intimate detail of how I was experiencing life without them in a faraway land. That hunger was likely beyond any possibility of being satisfied under the circumstances.

At the same time, almost every waking hour of our day was programmed, so I had little time to write. Besides, I was completely confused, beyond the language problems, by new and strange things I did not understand and was unable to put into writing. How could I tell my parents about new modes of penmanship? Different ways of using knives and forks? Having to break a piece of bread in half, putting half on the napkin ring, breaking the other half in two before buttering it? In short, I was in a weird new world.

Looking back now, my heart breaks when I think of those dear people, their lives in tatters, writing cheerful letters and cards to keep up the spirits of their little girl so far away. With no income and their assets frozen, they spent precious money on sending me my favorite chocolates and crayons, even my favorite comic magazines.

<u>May 27.</u>
Didn't you write even once this week? Did you ever receive the suitcase or Papagei and Kiebitz? Write <u>soon</u> and answer all my questions.
Mutti

Batzlein,
Did you receive the colored pencils and note paper? Answer our questions.
Happy Pentecost. Papi

When mothers and fathers or aunts and uncles came to visit the other boarders in my class, I would be sad that I was missing out on such family events. However, I consoled myself with a recurrent daydream:

My Mother and Father are walking up to the convent to come for me. As we are having a grand reunion, all the other girls are so envious of me once they see what a beautiful and distinguished family I have.

<u>May 28.</u>
It's good that you go to communion diligently and say your prayers. I am happy your English is going well. To make sure your skin problem goes away, use the skin cream in your toilet kit. Manschi is so happy that she'll be with you soon.
Pieperl, more kisses. Mutti

God will bless you for being devout and make everything turn out for the best—even when we don't see what the best for us is. With us, nothing new, so nothing to tell you. Tomorrow I try again to get passports, but fear they'll make me wait again. We may try to emigrate to somewhere else.
Papi

Cottages, Castles and Country Houses

At summer time and holiday vacations all the other girls left the boarding school to go home. I had no home to go to. What were the nuns supposed to do with me when other children went back to their families?

To address this challenge they figured out various things. They farmed me out to various friends or relatives of the nuns and lay teachers or sent me with my school-mates to be with their families. My mission often was to be a companion or governess to the children of families that took me in. Thus my times away from school afforded me intimate glimpses into a wide range of Scottish places and life styles.

My hosts included families of substantial wealth as well as families of extremely modest means—working folk as well as landed gentry. My old address book lists

people I met, including the Honorable Elizabeth Elphinston who lived in Carberry Tower, the castle above, and Lady Margaret Egerton who lived in Buckingham Palace!

The cottage above was sketched by Katherine Wright, a neighbor of the Highland cottage I stayed in. She wrote this poem beneath her sketch:

Poverty or boundless wealth, I know not which is best, But dwellers in a little house, Have often God as guest.

Miss McHardy

Craigellachie Hotel

Shipped Off to a Hotel

Six weeks or so after my arrival at the Queen's Cross boarding school, it was already summer. I spent that first vacation not in a home but in a lovely little hotel in the Highlands. It was in the village of Craigellachie on the banks of the River Spey. The hotel manager was a young lady, Miss McHardy, a cousin of one of the school nuns.

Fortunately for me, she agreed to let an Austrian ten-year-old who barely spoke English come stay with her.

June 27 1939.

Little Arkelein.

Lucky child, now you get to have a holiday in the Scottish Highlands. Enjoy yourself in the hotel. Be polite and pleasant to Miss McHardy.

Mutti

Bridge Across the Spey

How do you pronounce Craigellachie? Eat whatever you get, even if it isn't familiar, to be strong, tall and healthy. You were always Papi's round Batzlein and should stay like that. Sing, dance, play and be cheerful.   Papi

July 3.

The picture you drew of Craigellachie is very pretty. Having your own room is wonderful. Keep it tidy so everything doesn't lie about like cabbages and turnips. Sadly you still don't eat your porridge. Try some of it. Miss McHardy wrote that she will bring Anna McDonald from the village to play with you. Mutti.

It won't rain all the time. When the weather is nice, try to be outdoors. Don't read too much. When you swim outdoors, if the water is very cold, don't stay in the water too long, do you hear me? Be very obedient to Miss McHardy
Papi

Perhaps on the radio or from older people's conversation I heard something that made me nervous—or even sick—worrying about my parents. They assured me everything was fine then changed the subject, corrected my German and brought me up to date about my Viennese chum who was supposed to join me.

July 6.

Arkelein.
You don't need to get excited. Everything's quiet here and no one talks about war. You mustn't be afraid. You should write ent-ferent, not entfahrnt. Manschi has her passport but is missing tax papers and you know how difficult it is to get those.
Mutti

How can you be such a tschapperl [silly one] **and get upset about news without foundation? Don't worry about things you don't understand. Don't throw up over war news. Maybe you ate something hot before letting it cool down. Don't get excited unnecessarily. Enjoy the holiday, eat properly, sleep well.**

Be embraced by your Papilein.

Among the hotel guests I soon became everyone's pet. I seemed to pick up English rapidly during walks with my grown-up friend, Miss McHardy. On our walks I learned the English words for picnic and rabbit, and also heather, which happens to be what my name Erika means. The countryside near the hotel abounded in lots of heather and rabbits. Soon other words followed.

July 13.

It's two months since you left. Did you receive the lebkuchen? I go now to Mrs. Richards to give her daughter Manschi your card. In August a Kindertransport is supposed to take 12 children from the Swedish mission to Scotland; maybe Manschi will go with them. We still don't have our passports. We don't know where we can go. We are so grateful to Miss McHardy who wrote to her sister in New Zealand to see if they would take us.

Mutti

Miss Marshall lets you use her typewriter? Be grateful to her and take care not to damage her machine. Except for spelling errors, your letter was nicely written.

Papi

With friend Anna.

I also learned new words from children that Miss McHardy invited to play with me, probably with the purpose of hastening my language facility as well as for companionship. I sent photos of myself in Craigellachie to my parents. They noticed that I was putting on weight, thanks I suppose to generous helpings of the porridge that I finally forced down.

My new friend Anna McDonald unwittingly got me in trouble. Her family's cat had produced a litter. Since I had always wanted a pet, I was ecstatic when she offered me one of the cute kittens. I took it back to the hotel, not knowing that Miss McHardy thoroughly disliked cats and was allergic to them. In the hotel lobby was a nice couch. I sat there with my new pet, trying to put a bonnet on it and to tie a pretty ribbon around its neck. The poor creature was not at all pleased and showed it by peeing on the couch. Miss McHardy was even more displeased. She almost fainted when she came in and saw the kitten. She ordered me to return the animal immediately.

Undated.

You big dummy. How could you bring a cat into a stranger's house? You mustn't do such things. Beg forgiveness. Write and let us know that Miss McHardy has forgiven you and that things are okay between the two of you.
Mutti

Miraculously, by summer's end, while my parents were correcting me for my errors in German, I had become so comfortable with English that I returned to school ready to be in class with my peers, not the primary grades I had first been put in. Meanwhile, I must have written about missing my parents because my mother wrote, "You always want to know how far along we are with plans to leave. We asked for passports but still don't know when we shall get them. My little bunny rabbit, don't worry."

My father added, "You know how long these things take. We've been applying since May. Uncle Oskar Strakosch began in January and only just now got his passport."

A Modest Cottage in Braemar

Sheila Grant, one of my school friends, invited me to go home with her for many holidays. I presume now that the convent must have cleared this, or even arranged it, with her mother. At any rate, she lived in a beautiful little village called Braemar,

Above and below: Scenes around Braemar. Right: Scotland inspired me to paint.

nestled in a valley surrounded by hills—hills that inspired me to pull out my watercolor paints. Her family's modest cottage, like all the little houses, had names, not numbers, and the Grants' was called Havelock.

. The Grants treated me as one of their own. Sheila, close to my age, was the youngest of eight children, the only one still living at home. All the others, except one, lived within walking distance and some of them were always popping in. Being surrounded almost constantly by a houseful of brothers and sisters and feeling part of such a large family was a new and happy experience for me who had grown up without brothers or sisters.

Braemar on the River Dee is in the part of the Highlands known as the Cairngorms. The town is not far from Balmoral Castle where British royalty take their holidays every fall. The royals come to Braemar to attend the famous Highland Gatherings, an annual event in which Scots compete in sports and dancing. The scenery is breathtaking. The hills surrounding the athletic field are blazing with purple heather which covers them completely. The color is so bright as to be gaudy,

Mrs. Grant.

Mr. Grant

almost overdone like paintings on black velvet, yet wondrous to behold.

The competitions at the Games include some peculiarly Scottish sports. One is tossing the caber, a tree trunk that would appear nearly impossible to lift, let alone toss. Another is putting the stone, which amounts to heaving a rock weighing 16 to 28 pounds. Contests for who can do the best Scottish sword dance are always favorites. Mr. Grant officiated at times at these Games.

Prized family photos show him standing next to the queen and other members of the royal family at the opening ceremonies or while they are giving out awards. I could readily observbe that the Grants were highly respected and beloved members of their close-knit community.

In the summer Sheila and I would leave home after breakfast or lunch and not come back till dark. The world was ours, on foot or on bicycles. A long ride we loved was up to the Lynn of Dee, an exciting place where the river Dee races noisily through a narrow passage of solid rocks. We spent hours climbing hills, picking wild blueberries, fishing, catching tadpoles and hunting for firewood in the forest. Or we would lie in the heather daydreaming about what we would do when we grew up.

During Christmas holidays in Braemar, snow was something to revel in. Then sledding was my favorite sport.

With the Grants it seemed that everything happened in the kitchen. It was the warmest place in the cottage with its coal-burning

Sheila as adult at Havelock

stove. We all ate in the kitchen. Visitors came right into the kitchen. The kettle was always on and, whoever stepped over the threshold would be treated to a "fly cup" of tea—meaning on the run—and a home-baked scone to go with it. I don't remember a single day without a neighbor or one of the grown children stopping by. We even knitted in the kitchen. It was a comforting place.

There was a parlor too, but it was only used when the priest came to visit. The bedrooms were strictly for sleeping. The master bedroom for Mr. and Mrs. Grant was off the kitchen.

Like most homes in Braemar, ours did not have electricity. One of my chores was trimming the wicks of the paraffin lamps when it got dark. My bedroom was in the attic. The Scots are fond of stories about ghoulies and ghosties and in the flickering light it was easy to believe in these supernatural creatures. I dreaded the moment when it was bedtime and I had to go up to bed with a candle in hand. Afraid of ghosts lurking in the dark, I decided to pretend to be one of them myself—fooling them so they would leave a fellow ghost alone. Staring straight ahead with eyes wide open, I ascended step by step, thumping on each with what I hoped was ghostly mien, hardly daring to breathe until I reached the safety of the bed. Then came the most terrifying moment of all—time to blow out the candle. Rapidly pulling the covers over my head, I was finally safe.

Though well educated, the Grant family just survived economically. They rented their house, as did most villagers, from the laird who lived in a castle on a hill overlooking Braemar. Mr. Grant ran the village car repair garage, petrol station and bicycle rental business. Mrs. Grant raised her children, shopped, cooked, washed, gardened and saved money by raising chickens and gathering firewood in the woods behind the house.

During my many summer visits to Braemar I walked the short distance into the little village center. Often I would pass an old shepherd with his dog. I usually said good morning or hello. He said nothing. After several years of this attempted exchange, one fine day, after my "good morning" he replied, "Aye aye." A victory, I belonged. Recognized at last!

Once I got a phone call from the Braemar post woman who also ran the little grocery store in town. This was unusual in itself. Even more unusual, she said I had a telegram. "Not to worry," she said though. "It's nothing important."

The Grants' generosity and kindness to me, at a time when wartime scarcities made their lives even more precarious than usual, was nothing short of remarkable. At the time, however, I took it for granted. My doting parents and privileged upbringing back in Hohenau, always with maid service, led me to expect good things to come my way. I now recall with embarrassment times that I even took advantage of Sheila. After her mother asked us to do certain tasks around the house, I would tell Sheila, "You do the work and I'll make it look pretty." I must have been more spoiled than I like to recall.

The Chestnuts

If the Grant family in Braemar provided me with experiences with what might be thought of as the simple life among ordinary folk, the Reid family was my ticket to life with the upper crust in a castle and two elegant country houses, or mansions as they would be called in America.

Victoria Ingram was the mother of four little boys who lived with her mother, Lady Susan Reid, in a stately residence called The Chestnuts. It was in the small town of Ellon, about 16 miles north of Aberdeen. The house sits in a prominent location overlooking much of the town. Victoria's mother was known as "Old Lady Reid" to differentiate her from her daughter-in-law, Lady Tatiana Reid, who lived a few miles away in Ellon Castle.

I was a combination house guest and baby sitter for the Ingram boys. We read books together and played in the beautiful garden abounding with colorful flowers and a magnificent raspberry patch.

The interior of The Chestnuts was virtually a shrine to "Victoriana." Old Lady Susan had been a lady in waiting to Queen Victoria. Pictures of the queen were everywhere and many of them were signed, "Love, Vicky."

The Chestnuts had an illustrious history. Old Lady Reid's husband, the late Sir James Reid was Queen Victoria's physician. Sir James was also doctor to Ed-

The Chestnuts, Ellon.

The four Ingram boys who lived at The Chestnuts

ward VII and George V. It is said that Queen Victoria especially appreciated his prescription of kale as a laxative.

In the second half of 1914, Sir James was called to Scapa Flow where Prince Albert (later King George VI) had fallen ill while serving with Britain's grand fleet. The future king was taken to Aberdeen for surgery and, during his recovery, visited The Chestnuts on several occasions.

Ellon Castle

Another vacation was spent at Ellon Castle with Sir Peter and Lady Tatiana Reid and their two children. Sir Peter's father, Sir Edward Reid, was the son of the royal physician, Sir James Reid of The Chestnuts. Sir Edward had bought the castle in 1929.

My heart sank as I was driven up to the castle. The first thing that came into my view was a large mysterious-looking old ruin. I pictured myself spending my summer among ghosts in that forsaken place.

Fortunately the drive went on beyond the decrepit ruin. I was greatly relieved when we rode on and I saw the modern Ellon Castle, a fine structure that did not appear at all haunted.

While, I was there, Sir Peter spent most of his time in London so I have fewer recollections of him than of Lady Tatiana. Apparently it was typical at these large country homes for wives to be left in charge while husbands were in Parliament or on business trips for extended periods. Tatiana, of course, was not a Scottish name. Lady Tatiana was a White Russian and quite pretty.

I was a companion to their daugh-

ter Susan, about my age, and her younger brother, Peter, who was a student at Harrow, a prestigious public school which, in America, would be called a private school.

The Ellon Castle grounds had giant trees with large lower limbs spreading out so far it was a wonder they did not break. Along a stone wall was a long informal garden with a profusion of lupines, delphiniums, and other flowers of every size and color.

Clockwise from top: Ellon Castle; Susan and Peter at play with horse and cart; Susan in the garden; Peter in school uniform.

Letham House

Still another member of the Reid family, Jean Reid, invited me to spend a vacation at Letham House, her country mansion outside Haddington, near Edinburgh.

According to letters I wrote at

the time to my aunt and uncle in Ohio, which they saved, I was not easily impressed:

There is not much to tell. I am here with Mrs. Reid and the children. Every so often there is an outing to tea with some countess or lady so-and-so, but otherwise life is just the same, peaceful and contented evenings in the drawing room with Mrs. Reid while the wireless plays, the fire crackles and we chat about everything under the sun.

Another letter indicated I was still somewhat blasé:

I had lunch and tea with Lady Margaret Egerton, Princess Elizabeth's lady in waiting and a cousin of Mrs. Reid's. I have met and talked with the king's nephew and the queen's sister and niece. I liked them all at once. They are simple people, full of fun and most charming.

Simple people! It was at Letham House that I also met Lady Elphinstone who was lady in waiting to Queen Elizabeth, the mother of Queen Elizabeth II. She was nice enough to write a little note and to sketch a rabbit in my memory book—although that didn't endear me to her because she shot rabbits every chance she got.

Again I was supposed to be a companion to children, but I actually spent more time with Mrs. Reid. Once she took me to the grandest estate I had ever seen. It belonged to a duke and duchess. Their family name and that of their castle have faded from memory but the sense of wonder about the place remains. As I entered, the spaciousness made it feel like going into a cathedral. Suits of armor as if on guard were around the perimeter of the large circular entrance way.

Why I was brought along isn't clear to me now. I certainly did not drink the rum that was being served, or even the Coca Cola, which I don't believe I even tasted until I came to America. Perhaps I was being shown off as an Austrian refugee, but I really don't remember feeling that I was on display. By that time, as an early high school student, I was comfortable with adults, my manners were good by British or any standards, and English already felt like my native language.

On a Farm

One summer I went with another school friend, Erma Hector, to her home. She lived on a farm outside Buckie along the northeast coast of Scotland. Erma was beautiful with red hair and looked like she stepped right out of a Dante Gabriel Rossetti painting. Her parents had a dairy farm and a big black Labrador dog.

Sometimes we would pedal into town on our bikes. For a lark, we would let our pigtails loose—her red hair and my long black hair flowing in the wind. We usually wore our hair demurely braided, but when we let it loose on these occasions we felt utterly wicked, especially as we cycled past sailors on the wharf. If it was getting dark on our way home, we noticed sailors and young women in ditches beside the road. We would impishly shine our headlights on them as we raced by. Then we snickered and wondered what they were doing there.

Lossiemouth

We had more innocent pleasures. Erma and I tried so hard to invent a perfume from rose petals. We were completely unsuccessful as the petals turned rancid. We also spent hours lying on our backs in one special secret place that was completely covered with patches of wild forget-me-nots. We would stare at the clouds and day dream about our prince charming and how we would live happily ever after.

A treat was going to nearby Lossiemouth. It had a broad sandy beach, shown above, backed by rocky cliffs. There we swam in the North Sea. It was icy cold but we were young and apparently had enough blubber that it didn't matter and we enjoyed it thoroughly. How cold was it? When I took my husband there, years later, a seal popped its head out of the waves to watch us!

Mr. Hector was very tall with a red face and white hair, a genial giant. His wife was much younger and she would help entertain the soldiers stationed nearby. While she was merry, he often looked sad and solitary, and he seemed glad of our company.

Unlike most of my friends and classmates, the Hector's were not Catholic. But I recall one memorable Christmas, when Mr. Hector surprised our nuns by walking for miles with a Christmas tree and bringing it to them at the convent.

An Unhappy Seaside Vacation

Perhaps the only summer vacation that left me really sad was near Colliston, a seaside village on the east coast of Scotland, south of Aberdeen. I was invited to the summer cottage of a Lady Hudson and her two daughters, Rosemary and Elizabeth, both somewhat younger than I. I remember not particularly liking any of them.

There were high cliffs behind the house and I took walks on the moor above the cliff. Once a ship ran aground on the rock-bound shore, its hull ripped open and partially flooded. I watched lifeboats rescue crew members and passengers. This was big news in the local paper, which reported that the captain and four crew stayed on board awaiting help for salvaging cargo or possibly refloating the ship.

One day I was asked to take a baby for a walk in its carriage. Perhaps it was the child of a visitor. After I had gone a little while on my usual path on the moor above the cliffs, I suddenly realized the baby had kicked off one of its shoes. I looked and looked but couldn't find it. Whether because of an exaggerated sense of my failure, or perhaps because of repressed feelings about the course my life had taken, I felt desperate. I distinctly recall pondering about jumping off the cliff and ending it all.

I was only too happy to return to school.

Colliston—the harbor, the cliffs and the moor

Enjoying Solitary Confinement

As I grew older and gradually became aware that perhaps I was being farmed out as a charity case, I chose to spend several summer vacations at the convent in Aberdeen. Some might think that it was cruel and heartless that I was left in that large school all by myself. I ate alone. My meals were put out on a table by unseen people. I had practically no contact with any other children or adults.

Occasionally I saw the nuns playing tennis in the convent courts or walking quietly two by two, but mostly they were in their quarters and I in mine.

Actually, I reveled in my solitude. I had dominion over the library where I poured through books. I especially enjoyed the volumes of great art works. I devoured books about the unbelievable things that happened to the Christian martyrs, pierced by arrows or skinned alive—such horrible things that, today, I could no longer stomach. I had free reign of the beautiful gardens. Those long periods when I lived in happy isolation possibly explain why, throughout my adult life, I did not share the compulsion of many of my friends to be constantly surrounded by people. Rather, I had learned to greatly value and enjoy my complete privacy and a retreat from the company of others.

My Police Record

In Britain I was considered an "enemy alien." I had to check in with the police whenever I left Aberdeen, then register with the police at my destinations, and then check once more with the police on my return. I accepted this as the way things were

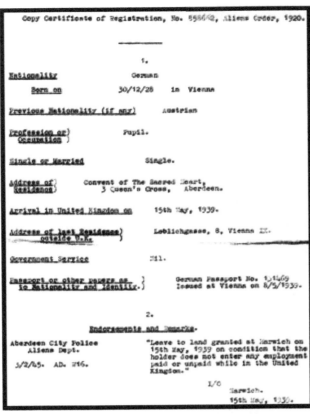

Copy Certificate of Registration, No. 858662, Aliens Order, 1920.

1.

Nationality — German

Born on — 30/12/28 in Vienna

Previous Nationality (if any) — Austrian

Profession or Occupation — Pupil.

Single or Married — Single.

Address of Residence — Convent of The Sacred Heart, 3 Queen's Cross, Aberdeen.

Arrival in United Kingdom on — 15th May, 1939.

Address of last Residence outside U.K. — Loblichgasse, 8, Vienna IX.

Government Service — Nil.

Passport or other papers as to Nationality and Identity — German Passport No. 1,1469 Issued at Vienna on 8/5/1939.

2.

Endorsements and Remarks.

Aberdeen City Police Aliens Dept.

3/2/45. AD. 716.

"Leave to land granted at Harwich on 15th May, 1939 on condition that the holder does not enter any employment paid or unpaid while in the United Kingdom."

I/O Harwich.
15th May, 1939.

'Dangerous Erika' whose every move was tracked by police [first of many pages of my British travel records]

done in this strange new land.

The irony did not strike me at the time. I was in Scotland because I had escaped persecution by the Germans. Yet, since Austria had been annexed to Germany, I arrived in Scotland with a German passport and so was classed as an enemy—as if I held allegiance to the nation that was putting my parents through hell.

Was this a peculiar time in a peculiar world or what?

Many Mothers—Sacred Heart Nuns

As weeks, then months and finally years went by without my parents' intended trip to Scotland to take me with them to America, 3 Queen's Cross became my home and, from 1939 to 1947, the nuns there were my family. Thanks to the sheltering granite walls and the loving attention of the Sacred Heart community, I felt secure.

I have already mentioned Mother MacLennan who mothered me and guided me on my arrival at the boarding school. The teaching nuns were called mothers, and I was fortunate to have many who became my family from the time I was ten until I left Queen's Cross convent and boarding school to go to college.

Four Outstanding Subjects

I have fondest memories of four subjects and four teachers at Queen's Cross. Those teachers were Mother MacPherson, Mother McDevit, Mother Curley, and Mother Horan. (They objected to being photographed in those days; the one shown below of Mother Horan was possibly taken surreptitiously.)

Mother MacPherson and Chivalry. Most of our nuns were Irish because they came from a nation that was a major Catholic stronghold. In Scotland, Protestants dominated and Catholics were a distinct minority. Mother MacPherson was one of the few Scottish nuns at our convent. She introduced us to medieval chivalry as if we were part of that ancient order. Each of us in our small class of eight or ten students had to earn our way up to knighthood.

We started as pages. Meanwhile we were being inculcated in the virtues that the knights supposedly practiced—courtesy, service, protecting the poor, noble bearing, valor and championing against evil. Each stage between page and knight had to be earned by conquering our many faults. What faults? Well, like talking or not sitting up straight or producing untidy homework. Thanks to Mother MacPherson, we took chivalry very seriously. Yet at the same time she made it a lot of fun.

Mother McDevit and French. Mother McDevit was very beautiful. This led us girls to concoct stories about why she had become a nun. We couldn't imagine such a beautiful young woman not having suitors and wonderful offers of marriage.

She was a good French teacher and was a stickler for learning an extensive vocabulary. Since the Sacred Heart was originally a French order, learning to speak French was deemed special and essential.

I remember that on one test we had a sentence including the words *canne à pêche*. One of my classmates hadn't done her homework. Instead of translating it as a fishing pole, she guessed and read it as "a can of peaches." We thought it was very funny, but Mother McDevit did not appreciate it and was not amused.

Mother Curley and Home Economics. Mother Curley taught sewing and other homemaking skills. She was very devoted to a favorite hero of hers, Saint Stanislaus, the patron saint of Poland. So while we were learning and practicing different stitches in class, she would have students take turns reading a book about this saint's life. After many readings, we became thoroughly bored with the story, and took great pleasure in skipping whole chapters at a time. She didn't seem to notice and we girls felt conspiratorially triumphant.

Mother Horan

Mother Curley was a meticulous teacher. As a result, when I became an adult and homemaker, on many occasions when I was sewing or cooking or examining the quality of clothes I was buying for my family, I had many occasions to appreciate what I had learned under Mother Curley's tutelage.

Mother Horan—Literature and Plays. My dearest memories are of Mother Horan who taught English, literature, Shakespeare and composition. She was so knowledgeable about her subject, so enthusiastic and so entertaining that it was a joy to be in her classes. We hated when the bell rang. She made the books and plays we read come alive. We could hardly wait till her next class.

In those days I really looked forward to Mother

Horan's weekly essay assignment. I did well, got good grades on them, but often with a note: "Pithy." One of my best friends, but a rival competing for best marks, was Joan Henry. Her writing was full of big words and rather convoluted. Not pithy. When Joan got better grades, I liked to

Barbara Clarke, Erika [age 14], Alice Riddle in "In the Name of the Queen."

think it was because no one wanted to admit they didn't understand her essays.

Mother Horan was in charge of all types of dramatics. Those who know me as an adult who shuns the limelight may find it hard to believe that as a student nothing thrilled me more than being stage center and confidently showing off my talents.

As an indication of Mother Horan's caring personality, she kept in touch with our whole class after graduation. At Christmas time she waited until after she had heard from each of us. Then, in what she called her round robin, she would compile and share the news of our jobs, weddings, husbands, children, interesting trips, events happy or sad, all interspersed with bits of philosophy about life and memories of odd things that happened during our plays at Queen's Cross. Amazingly, these cherished round robins from Mother Horan continued, year after year, almost until she died. She retired back to her native Ireland where we visited her twice in the little town of Armagh—first with my husband, our two sons, and my husband's parents, and second, just with my husband but joined by another classmate, Gella Culhane, who came from Northern Ireland for a touching reunion with us and Mother Horan.

Habits

Especially when we were very young and new to the boarding school, the nuns were a great mystery to us. Their skirts touched the floor so we couldn't see their shoes. Did they have feet like regular people? Or did they waft about so smoothly because they were on wheels? Our Sacred Heart nuns wore a wimple tight around their face. We never saw their hair and tried to guess if they had any or what color hair they might have.

In my days with them, the nuns at our school were cloistered, rarely leaving the convent. Their religious order was immediately recognizable from their distinctive habits. This changed of course after Vatican II in 1962 when some of the Sacred Heart nuns donned "civilian" clothes and moved about freely in the communities where they were located.

I should add that it was my special good fortune to be sent to a Sacred Heart school. The teaching nuns were exceptionally well trained. Some have characterized them as the female version of the Jesuits. Starting with the original Sacre Coeur in France, they tended to cater to daughters of upper class families. Whether it was true in their schools throughout the world, the nuns in Aberdeen were uncommonly kind and loving, in counterpoint to their strictness in inducing their charges to aim for the highest standards of conduct and learning.

Not all the nuns in our convent were known as mothers. The non-teaching nuns, known as sisters, did the cooking, cleaning and other every-day chores. My recollection is that most of these sisters were from Ireland. They were second class nuns in a sense. Yet, considering the poverty, hunger, illness and abuse that were the lot of too many young Irish women in the first half of the nineteen hundreds, their acceptance into the Sacred Heart community was to them an escape to relative abundance in a safe, healthful, respectful and secure place.

Mother Paterson

It was Reverend Mother Paterson, the headmistress, who greeted me on my arrival at the convent. She was chosen by my parents as my guardian to see about my precollege education until—as they and I fervently hoped—they would come for me. My parents in Vienna kept in touch with Mother Paterson by mail from the start until their deportation. They were reassured as she wrote them about my progress. I trusted her completely, went to her for advice and loved her very much. I kept in touch with her until she died.

A Famous Relative Appears

One day, four years after I had been at Queen's Cross, Reverend Mother Paterson sent for me to come see a visitor who was waiting for me. You can imagine how excited I was.

Soon standing in front of me in the convent parlor was someone I had heard about but had never met before—an imposing figure, six feet tall with curly black hair and a courtly manner.

Nothing could have been more improbable than that Victor Moritz Goldschmidt, known to associates as V.M., and known to me as Uncle Victor, would come to live and work in Aberdeen where I was living. Pulling the unlikely threads of this story together is reminiscent of a Dickens novel.

Our Norway Connection

My parents wrote:

> **August 28, 1939.**
>
> **Arkelein,**
>
> **Mail won't go between here and Scotland any more. Write to Uncle Victor:**
> **Prof. Dr. Victor Goldschmidt, Holmenkollen, Oslo, Norway.**
>
> > **Mutti and Papi**

> **September 9, 1939.**
>
> **This letter will probably take a long time to travel to you. Listen my little one about the detour to Uncle Victor. Address letters to him and he will send them on to us.**
>
> **Your friend Manschi is very unhappy she cannot come to you now. About**

us, you don't need to worry. We're both well. With God's help we will live through the war. Mutti

My little Darling,
Unfortunately it wasn't possible to get our passports on time, so we must stay here. Pray that the Lord will let us see each other again. Now it will take a long time before your letters arrive. Write clearly so the censor won't hold them up.
      Papi

World War II had begun in earnest. Previously Hitler's Germany had gobbled up Austria, the country from which I had escaped but where my parents were stuck. In September of the year I came to Aberdeen the Nazis invaded Poland. Britain in response declared war on Germany. Suddenly it became impossible for me to send letters directly to my parents, or they to me. To put it another way, my parents and I were now living in opposing camps.

This turn of events gave me a rationale for accepting the fact that my parents' plans to join me and take me to America were not about to occur. Clearly those plans would have to wait until the war ended. My parents spared me from worrying about their fate by writing repeatedly that they were fine and everything was in order, except for what they led me to believe were inconsequential problems and delays in getting travel documents.

In any event, my parents urged me to send mail to them via Uncle Victor, a first cousin of my father and an eminent scientist who was a professor of geochemistry in Oslo. Norway was still neutral at this time. We did exchange some letters to each other by this round-about route, as well as by way of Switzerland via another cousin of my father's, Steffi Habig, who had fled there from Vienna.

Our writing plan worked for a time, until April 8, 1940 when the Nazis invaded Norway. My parents' letters dwindled. On rare occasions I received cryptic messages from them via the Red Cross. Not only did Germany's conquest of Norway break our communication scheme. Much worse, as I learned long afterwards, it prevented my parents from escaping to Norway as they and Uncle Victor had been planning. It was one of many, many "almost ways out" of Austria and Hitler's domain that fell through for my parents.

Narrow Escape

Even before the invasion, a virulently anti-Semitic group of Nazi sympathizers in Norway was compiling records of people of Jewish heritage in their country. The infamous Vidkun Quisling, a Norwegian politician and then president after the invasion, was so welcoming to Hitler's forces that freedom lovers—in his country and around the world—began calling all traitors "quislings." The Norwegian Nazis handed over their lists of Jews who were quickly rounded up by the conquering Germans. They took Uncle Victor prisoner.

Norway also had its resistance fighters. Among them were some of Goldschmidt's scientific colleagues and admirers. They managed to rescue him at the port moments before he was to be put aboard a ship. A book recounting the history of Norway in World War II tells that his fellow prisoners who did not share his fortune of being rescued were put on that ship and taken to be exterminated at the Auschwitz concentration camp.

Unsafe in Oslo, Victor fled from Norway in a horse-drawn wagon under a load of hay, crossing the Norwegian border into Sweden. His reputation preceded him and the university in Stockholm immediately offered him the chair of the science department. He declined, however, because he was determined to help in the war effort against Germany. The Swedes cooperated and enabled him to find safe passage to Great Britain.

Happy Twist of Fate

By an amazing coincidence, Victor was stationed at the Macaulay Institute, not far from the Queen's Cross Convent in Aberdeen where I was a boarding pupil. Victor was really my second cousin, but I called him uncle because he was in his fifties and I was only fourteen.

Why was Uncle Victor located so far from the joint English and United States war command headquarters in London? Here's what I learned decades later. There was strong suspicion in innermost circles that the Germans, like the Allies, were trying to create an atomic bomb. Victor, collaborating with Einstein and others, was in the forefront of discoveries about heavy water and other atomic matters. Victor, once in England, began exuberantly sharing his findings with other scientists. Military officials who were tapping into his advanced discoveries about the nature of elements feared that his openness might leak secrets to enemy agents. So they posted him to this rather remote corner of Scotland where he could pursue his work clandestinely, securely away from probing eyes and ears.

Overcoming Barriers of Language, Age and Interests

Especially at first, our conversations were halting. My uncle's English was not very good. He was born in Zurich, Switzerland in 1888. He had been the founding director of a mineralogy institute in Göttingen, Germany, so he was very fluent in German. However, he apparently did not want to speak German because of his terrible experiences with the Nazis, which I did not know at the time because he told me nothing of that. Besides, since I had not spoken a word of German during my four years in Scotland, my German was rusty, almost nonexistent.

Yet it was a wonderful feeling to know that, like all of my schoolmates, I finally had a real live relative nearby.

From time to time Uncle Victor brought me to afternoon tea where he lived. With pride, he would show me different equations he had worked out and that were spread out on two very large work tables. I was still having trouble with arithmetic and possibly tried to look impressed, but I had no idea what his work was all about.

Other times he would invite me for a walk. Occasionally we went to the Rubislaw Quarry in the west end of Aberdeen. Even behind the fence marked with DANGER signs, for anyone afraid of heights, this granite quarry was scary. Roughly the size of two football fields, it was over 465 feet deep, one of the deepest man-made holes in Europe. From the mid-1700s it had provided building material for most Aberdeen structures, including our convent, which explains why Aberdeen is known as the Granite City. Giant elevators and pulleys took workers down and brought up to street level the blocks of granite that ended up in prominent buildings such as the Parliament in London. After World War II, quality stone was no longer found so quarrying stopped and the huge excavation pit became filled with water.

A Passion for Animals

Uncle Victor also took me to sheep dog trials. The amazing dogs, responding to signals from their masters, would swiftly corral flocks of sheep along a prescribed course. My uncle's love of animals, like that of his father's, went back to his days in Oslo. A biographer had fun recalling something of this aspect of his life:

The household, in addition to its human inhabitants, consisted of the famous dachshund "Bazi"—which tyrannized father and son; three squirrels demanded and received a home in the bathroom; a toad hibernated in the cellar, and a family of bats resided in the loft. Each had a name, and the toad shared his name with a well-known and not too endearing character in Göttingen. One of the squirrels was named Parsifal (because, V.M. said, he was indescribably stupid), another was Richard, but the most notorious squirrel was Magdalena who came to a sad and untimely end. V.M. gave a birthday party for Bazi and several dog guests were invited to share the birthday cake. In the excitement, Bazi concluded on this special day everything was permitted and ended the feast by devouring Magdalena. [From chapter on Goldschmidt, by Paul Rosbaud, in _Great Chemists_, E. Farber, editor, John Wiley & Sons, 1961.]

Scientific Honors

I was unaware of how very famous my uncle was until he was awarded an honorary degree at the University of Aberdeen.

Victor's achievements later earned him the 1944 Wollaston Medal, the highest honor in his field. The Geochemical Society to this day presents an annual honor award in Goldschmidt's name. Brian Mason, a New Zealander who had been a student of Victor's in Oslo, eventually became a specialist on the composition of meteors with the Smithsonian Institution in Washington. He wrote a biography about my uncle in 1992, _Victor Moritz Goldschmidt, Father of Modern Geochemistry._

I was extremely pleased to meet Brian and hear his tales of Uncle Victor. When Brian came to dinner with us, he was taken aback—startled and even more delighted—to find himself using silverware that had been passed down to me with the initials SG, standing for Salomon Goldschmidt, a common ancestor of mine and Victor's.

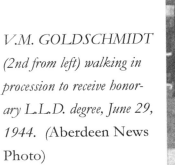

V.M. GOLDSCHMIDT (2nd from left) walking in procession to receive honorary L.L.D. degree, June 29, 1944. (Aberdeen News Photo)

A Femme Fatale in His Life

After some time, V.M. left Aberdeen and continued his work at the Rothamsted Experimental Station near Harpendon, England. He made frequent trips from there to London and on one of my vacations I spent time with him at a London hotel. His fiancé was also staying there, and I shared her hotel room.

Her name was Sis Gruner-Hegge, with whom Uncle was besotted. I was probably there as a kind of chaperone—which was quite a joke since, as an extremely sheltered school girl, I knew nothing of the ways of the world of adults. To illustrate that fact, it did not seem strange to me that Sis was rarely in my room.

At any rate, Uncle Victor credited Sis with helping him escape from Norway to Sweden, and she gave him hope by talking to him of a divorce from her husband who was none other than the conductor of the Oslo Philharmonic.

The short time I experienced in the hotel with Sis was full of questions—questions about her relationship to Uncle Victor, among others. We had no language in common and I worshipped her from afar. She was in her thirties, very pretty, dressed in only the most expensive clothes. Most wondrous to me, she used make-up and wore perfume, things totally foreign to an unsophisticated girl confined to life in a convent. When all I knew were blue knickers and white undershirts, it was an eye-opening thrill for me to see her array of frilly lacy undergarments.

I learned years later that Sis had used Victor to get to England where she was in pursuit of yet another lover. Victor eventually thanked fate for sparing him from marrying someone with whom he was incompatible in things most important to him.

In My Uncle's Circle

One of the many good things about Uncle Victor coming into my life was that he let me get to know a number of his friends in Scotland and England.

While Victor was at Rothamsted, he introduced me to the Ogg family. Sir William Ogg was director of the world-renowned agricultural experimental station there and became a very

Einstein, in black coat, on geological field trip with V.M. in Norway.

close friend to both Uncle Victor and me, as did his wife, Lady Ogg.

Once they invited me there for a vacation. A high point was a visit with them to Hadrian's Wall—built by the Romans during their occupation of Britain to separate northern England from the barbarians, that is, the Scots! The Oggs and I kept in touch throughout the years. Long after I had left Scotland, I returned in 1967 for a lovely visit at the Ogg's estate. There Sir William and his wife entertained me, my children, my husband and my husband's parents.

One of V.M.'s colleagues was Albert Einstein who visited him in Norway where V.M. taught him to sail. I never met Einstein, but Uncle Victor introduced me to another colleague and admirer, Max Born and his wife. They had also found refuge in Britain. Sad to say, I did not fully appreciate meeting a future Nobel laureate in those days. One letter from my parents urges me to be sure to thank Mrs. Born for sending

Playing with the Singers' wolf hound

me a package of goodies at school. Touchingly, despite the many miles separating us and the growing time from seeing each other, my mother and father never stopped trying to perfect my behavior.

Dr. Felix Singer, a patent attorney for Uncle Victor's inventions, lived outside London in Croydon. I spent some time with that family too. I enjoyed being with their daughter who was my age, and I was impressed with their enormous Russian wolf hound.

Morality and Philosophy

I got the impression that Victor enjoyed talking with the nuns at my school, and they with him. I wish I could have heard their discussions of religion and philosophy. Victor had not been a practicing Jew. But the Nazi's anti-Jewish policies became evident while he was teaching in Göttingen in the 1930s. It tells a lot about his character that he reacted by proudly affirming his heritage and joining a synagogue.

Although Uncle Victor had a signed letter from Hitler and Goering permitting him to return to Norway in 1935, he was nevertheless put in a concentration camp for a time. He urged two fellow prisoners to join him in remembering the names of their torturers. Uncle Victor was surprised by their responses. One, a pious Jew, said, "Revenge is not for us; that must be left to the Almighty." The other, an atheist, said, "We must break the evil circle of retribution, or there can never be an end to evil."

These objections to his call for vengeance made a deep impression on him. In one of his last letters to his friend Paul Rosbaud—a German metallurgist who worked for the Nazis while secretly keeping the Allies informed of Germany's failed atomic bomb attempts—V.M. wrote that he felt these principles cited by his two fellow prisoners were "even more important than my contributions to scientific and industrial research. To set a new standard of morality," he continued, "is a matter of great urgency in these times."

I can well imagine that he discussed such matters with the nuns.

Something else that he discussed with me has stuck in my memory. He stressed that the two most important things in life are, first, having two real friends and, second, having good health. At the time that struck me as truly strange.

As to friends, I felt that to have only one or two friends was to be almost alone. At age 14, of course, I did not know the difference between playmates and real friends, even though I usually had a couple special friends. Years later I realized what Uncle Victor meant by "real friends"--those who are genuine soul mates who care deeply about each other, not merely casual acquaintances.

As to health, young people naturally take good health for granted, if they have it, as I did most of the time. It is well documented that Uncle Victor, on the other hand, had more than his share of serious illnesses throughout his life. These, along with the shocks to his system from imprisonment and a second capture by the Nazis, his arduous escape to Sweden and then to Britain, plus his enormous drive to push forward with his pioneering scientific ventures in the face of physical and political hurdles, surely contributed to his early death.

Shortly after World War II ended, Uncle Victor returned to his beloved Norway. Not long after, in 1947, he died at age 59.

Contribution to Geochemistry

To the extent I understand my uncle's place in science, I believe he did for the physical world what Darwin did for the living world. That is, he showed how all elements and compounds evolved from a common source, their atomic structures altered by heat, pressure, radiation and other forces. He undertook the complex analysis of how the elements are distributed on earth.

In support of the war effort, I learned that he helped determine likely landing spots for the invasion of Europe by Allied troops. His knowledge of geology enabled him to calculate the ability of various French beaches to sustain and accommodate the weight of tanks and other heavy equipment.

Apparently few in the scientific community of his era understood the importance

of his findings and theories. But as time went on, some of his disciples won Nobel prizes for carrying on Victor's work. He wrote about the effect of man-made carbon dioxide on the atmosphere back in 1936, anticipating modern concerns about global warming. He also undertook groundbreaking studies of the chemical causes of silicosis.

His prodigious experiments and writings appear all the more remarkable in light of his personal history. A whole floor of the natural history museum in Oslo is dedicated to his life and his work. Norway in 1974 honored his achievements further by picturing Goldschmidt on a postage stamp, shown here.

Leaving Me with Hope

Uncle Victor returned to Oslo and I never saw him again. I now have evidence that, before he left, he knew or at least strongly suspected the fate of my parents. However, there was no definite news of them. Rather, there was a complete absence of news. So that kind man probably did not want to be the one to take away my hope that I would somehow be reunited with my mother and father.

War in the Eyes of Youngsters

Imagine school girls during World War II seeing buildings with walls missing and hardly thinking about the poor families that had been bombed out. Or imagine us wishing for another air raid. Looking back, our child's vision of the war seems mighty peculiar and insensitive.

It is perhaps less odd in light of our upbringing and the environment created for us. We rarely listened to the radio or read newspapers. Television did not exist. Parents and teachers in the circles we grew up in were in what might be called a protective mode. They talked to us about childish things, seldom sharing realities and concerns of their adult world. My schoolmates and I therefore enjoyed a distancing from reality that is hard to conceive in today's world of round-the-clock headline news and television images of mayhem, sex and ugliness from which modern youngsters can hardly escape.

Happy-go-lucky classmates: Angela Rice, Joan Henry, Patricia Dempsey, Gella Culhane, Patsy Mullen and Erika

Air Raids

Once World War II began in 1939, Aberdeen, an important port city, was itself a German target. Our city was also directly on the path that Nazi bombers flew from Norway to London, their principal target.

The nuns prepared for emergencies by issuing us gas masks. We each had to wear one in a packet, like a camera case, when we went out on walks. We often took rather long walks from the convent. After bombing raids we would pass houses with the sides knocked out. Beds, wardrobes, dining rooms and so forth were exposed to our view. Yet to the best of my memory we did not connect what we saw with the fact that people in those places had suffered, been injured or might even have been killed.

When there was an air raid warning, we took our gas masks along when we headed to shelter. It was a small room in the convent basement, a room with no windows. The raids usually came at night. We learned to be very quick in getting downstairs and taking our assigned seats. We were very crowded there and more than a little uncomfortable.

Praying for the Next Raid

To keep us from being afraid, the nun in charge would distract us by reading from an interesting book. As soon as the all-clear sounded, the book was slammed shut and we had to go upstairs and get quickly back to bed. Typically the story was very exciting and the suspense was so great that we would actually pray for an air raid the next night so we could continue to hear the rest of the story.

If the all-clear after a night-time raid came before midnight, we had to rise at the usual 6:30 a.m. But if the all-clear didn't sound until after 12, we were allowed to sleep an extra hour. Again, thinking only of ourselves and not of damaged buildings or endangered lives, we prayed with all our fervor that the all-clear would be delayed.

Defense in a Tiny Village Was No Joke

When I was with Sheila at the Grants, blackouts were ordered even in Braemar despite the fact that the tiny and remote Highland village was an unlikely target. Mr. Grant was an air raid warden, a role he took very seriously. He would walk around the village to make sure no chink of light was showing through the villagers' blackout blinds, no light to guide enemy pilots coming to bomb us.

At times, news came over the radio that enemy planes were headed our way. When the air raid warning sounded, all of the women—as many as four at a clip—put on fur coats and then piled into the bed in the master bedroom, waiting for the all-clear.

In case Braemar was invaded, people were ready to head for the hills with pitch-forks or whatever they could use to defend themselves. Anticipating that the German army might come their way, the Scots tore down road signs at junctions, or changed them to point in the wrong directions to confuse any invaders.

In retrospect, this may seem humorous. It was nothing to joke about at the time. Thankfully, the invasion never happened. Yet Britain might well have been overrun by the Germans if Hitler and his commanders had not made their mistake, fatal to them, of going in the opposite direction in an attempt to conquer the Soviet Union.

Sobs in the Night

Little fragments gave us momentary but disconnected snapshots of the course of the war. One night in the convent a girl was crying as we were being put to bed. The nun in charge of the dormitory comforted her and asked her what the matter was. Between sobs, the girl said, "Paris has fallen!" I recall being puzzled about what that meant, how she knew it, or how it affected us.

A Death Struck Home

At Queen's Cross we had a number of lay teachers. One was a music teacher. She was quite pretty and had recently been married. Her husband was sent to fight and then became one of the early war fatalities. Hearing about that did affect us girls and we felt terribly sad for our teacher.

Love Conquers All

War could not compete with or interfere with my first romance. In my early teens I fell in love with Frederic Chopin, alias actor Cornel Wilde. Our class had taken a field trip to see the movie, "A Song to Remember." Transported by the music and emo-tionally high-jacked by the vision of the tubercular composer's blood spattered on the piano keys, I succumbed to my first love.

Because the nuns read all of our outgoing and incoming mail, I secretly smuggled a letter to be mailed outside the convent to my hero, Cornel Wilde. Years later, I saw Tchaikovsky's opera, "Eugen Onegin," in which a naïve young Tatiana writes a frenzied declaration of her love. I identified immediately with that letter-writing scene. I never heard back from Wilde so he missed his chance to know me. Seriously, though, I did learn how powerful music can be and how fortunate those of us are who find its magic weave its spell for us as a life-long and life-giving first love.

Days of Terror

Our chief fears in those days were unrelated to the war we were living through. Our days of terror were when the roving Scottish supervisors came to test us. Our school, like all schools, had to meet standards that applied throughout Britain. None of my classmates could forget the near panic with which we anticipated the periodic visits of Ms. McGlashen who inspected our sewing and other domestic science work. Nor could we forget the nervousness of our teachers who did not want us to fail—a nervousness compounded because they themselves were being judged by the national supervisor. Our instructors tried valiantly to prepare us for tough science and math questions. And I recall a literature teacher advising us: if we were unsure about the identity of a quotation, it was a good idea to guess that it came from either the Bible or Shakespeare.

Not to Worry

As the war continued, I got one of the infrequent letters from my parents. They informed me that they had moved out of my grandmother's apartment to another apartment in the center of the city of Vienna. I learned later that this was the ghetto-izing of Austrian Jews who had been dispossessed of their apartments and most of their possessions. It was a kind of collection point so it would be easier to gather them up and force them onto trains to Poland, but I was given no indication of that at the time.

Fragments of various letters from my parents that follow reveal their efforts to keep me in childish ignorance or focused on mundane things:

July 28, 1939,

My Dear Arkelein,

How can you be in such despair when you have to wait for our mail? The blame is not ours but with the postal service and censors who let letters lie around. We are both well. You mustn't worry about us. Write: what are you learning now?

You mustn't be upset about being separated from us. It's a test God has made and you have to accept it. We all hope we will be reunited. Be patient and thank God you are with such nice people in a wonderful convent. Your hen-scratching writing was naughty with bad spelling and grammar. I hope you are well and happy but you're a lazy good-for-nothing to leave us so long without news.

I [mother] just took a class to make neckties and I made a few beautiful ones.

I [father] am taking a class in analyzing blood so I can do something different…than making sugar when I go abroad. Try to play the piano a little.

Perhaps we get our passport next week, but what we will do then we still do not know. How did you learn to ride a bike?

      Mutti and Papi

A Memorable Time with Actors

One winter during the war years, no one had invited me for the Christmas holidays. The enterprising nuns found a solution for me.   I was to travel to various isolated villages throughout the Highlands with a troupe of actors who were going to perform there.

This unlikely opportunity came about because of Tina Megroz who was ahead of me a few years at school. Tina was a relative of the English author and poet Walter de la Mare, and she had already been engaged to go along with this troupe, so the nuns worked it out that I could join her.

The leader of this small but stalwart acting group was Ann Casson, whose mother was the world-famous actress, Dame Sybil Thorndike (for whom George Bernard Shaw wrote his play, Saint Joan).   I don't recall much about our group's plays, but one magical evening on this tour with them stands out and remains fresh in my mind.

We were driving through the countryside and everything was covered with snow and ice. The night was pitch black, no twinkle of light anywhere. Blackout regulations made sure of that. We were cold and hungry when we arrived at our destination, a farmhouse far from any other human habitation.

As we stepped through the door, it was as if we had arrived in heaven. An enormous table took center stage. On it was food, lots of it. Heaps of eggs, meat, butter, jams, homemade oatcakes and more. These were all things we had not seen in a long time because of rationing. A blazing fire warmed our frozen toes while the marvelous feast warmed our tummies and our hearts.

Taking Whatever Comes Along

It has frequently been observed that children accept pretty much anything that comes along because they have no perspective of what alternatives life could offer. This was certainly true for me and my friends during the war years in Scotland.

Looking back, the war to us meant two bad things—poor food (which explains why my tour with the actors was so memorable) and awful cold. The best food was sent to the fighting forces, civilians got the dregs. Imagine that in Scotland, surrounded by water, our fish was so fishy that I thought I hated fish. It was a revelation later to find out how delicious fresh fish could be. Fresh fruit was rare too. As to the temperature, the convent, like other places, cut way back on heating. I and others got chilblains. Our knuckles would get red and split open. Bandages covered a salve and I had to wear gloves to cover the bandages. Tips of the fingers of the gloves were cut off so I could hold pens or pencils. At those painful times I would take an oath never to get cold again—and I still don't like the cold.

How innocent and naïve were we as young teenagers? One of the many war-time songs sung by the soldiers that we heard coming over the radio was a jolly tune we girls picked up. With abandon we sang lustily, "Roll me over in the clover, roll me over, lay me down and do it again." I doubt any of us knew what that song was really about!

War Ends, Boarding School Ends—Then What?

I come to another blackout period in my life. The first blackout was during my journey from Vienna to Aberdeen. That trip on a Kindertransport to England, then by train north to Scotland, lasted three days. The journey saved my life but most of it remains a complete blank to me.

The second blackout is measured not in days but years - actually two years in Edinburgh. Most of that period has disappeared from my memory.

End of an Era for the World, and for Me

It was 1946. World War II had ended in the Pacific, a year after Hitler's defeat in Europe. I had not heard from my parents since late 1941. In 1944 one of the Aberdeen priests tried through the Vatican to get news of them. But no word.

My mother's sister and her husband, my Aunt Mia and Uncle Fritz Treuer, had escaped in 1938 via England to America. Through correspondence, I had been in close touch with them. From my earliest days at the convent they wrote that they wanted me to come to them in Ohio.

That was impossible. The nuns felt obliged to let me finish at boarding school as they had promised my parents. Yet they agreed I should then join my American family and they promptly approved my applying for a United States visa. For years and years I tried unsuccessfully to get that visa. American consuls in Glasgow and London kept stalling. Time after time I was told everything was just about in order. On one occasion money was sent so I could make reservations on a ship or on a Dutch airline. But officials always found something missing. No birth certificate, so I had to write relatives in London and Switzerland to send sworn statements about the date and place of my birth. No affidavits from Americans affirming they would not let me be a financial burden to their country, so Aunt Mia obtained those and sent them to me. After more delays by the consul, he said those affidavits were out of date and had to be renewed. When all

I needed was the visa, he claimed my number had not come up—my number under an Austrian quota. Then I had to apply for a certificate of identity. An attorney of Uncle Victor's, a Mr. Paull in Aberdeen, wrote tons of letters to try to expedite the matter.

The convent and my aunt and uncle begged Catholic, Evangelical and Jewish refugee organizations to speed things up, with no luck. I went myself by train to the American consulate in Glasgow. After arriving there for my appointment, I was told the consul was in America and his assistant was too busy to see me. Excerpts of two letters I wrote to my Aunt and Uncle during my last year at the Sacred Heart boarding school reveal my mix of despair and hope as official promises that all the paperwork was completed fell through.

April 22, 1946

I am almost at my wits end as to what to do to speed up the consul. I have all my papers, passport and passage, but NO VISA. Oh, I don't know what I am going to do if I can't come to you soon. All the nuns and I are praying hard—and so I hope <u>something</u> will happen.

June [no day] 1946

I am just broken-hearted, now when at last everything seemed settled. I am so sorry to have to disappoint you again. However, there is still hope and all is not lost.

I was finishing high school. At our graduation we had a very emotional parting. It was not easy for us to say goodbye. Our very close circle of girl friends had been living, studying and playing together for about eight years and now it was over. The others were going home or getting ready for college. Where was I to go?

Nobody said anything to me about my real situation. They didn't tell me I was an orphan, penniless, without family, free-floating and anchorless. When the war in Europe ended, Uncle Fritz and Aunt Mia wrote me to expect the worst about my parents. I found a copy of this letter in Mia's files after she died in 1990. The nuns, apparently not wanting me to read what was not a certainty, intercepted that letter and I am absolutely certain that they never let me see it.

I have also found copies of correspondence between various adult relatives—some of them early on from my parents—with a consistent theme concerning the horrors of the times and what they were all going through. That theme was a conspiracy of silence, as spelled out literally in some of the letters with these words, "Don't tell the child."

Having grown up in a privileged household and having been cared for in the convent boarding school, quarantined from the real world, it rarely occurred to me to think of a job. That was what common folk did, I supposed. That did not matter. Even had I wanted to work, my classification as an "enemy alien" prohibited me from taking a job in Britain in those days.

Get Me to a Nunnery

I decided that I should become a nun! The Sacred Heart community was my home, my life, my security. It was the one thing I knew. It was my life jacket while I was bobbing around in the water. I was very comfortable with the spiritual life and I was truly devout. It was the layer of reality that I knew.

When I shared my wish to become a nun with Reverend Mother Paterson, she must have been astounded. She replied quite calmly that I may or may not have a vocation to become a nun. Nevertheless, she said it was very important that I first "live in the world for a while." Wisely, she advised me that if, after that, I still felt strongly about becoming a nun, we could talk about it then and take it from there. She was so right. I did not have a vocation. I was lost, in limbo, rudderless, desperately looking for something to hang onto.

A Decision Is Reached—Craiglochart

I don't know whether my parents had a written contract or just an understanding with Mother Paterson about me. Had they or Aunt Ella Popper made some financial arrangement to cover my costs at the school? Had the convent promised to take care of me until my parents picked me up or until I finished school? My Uncle Victor was generous to a fault to all his friends and very loyal to his family. Had he perhaps given the convent a sum of money to provide for me? Did my aunt and uncle in America, who exchanged letters with the nuns, make recommendations about what I should

Craiglochart College.

do? All these are questions that now puzzle me but that can never be answered.

In any event, it was somehow determined that I would go to Craiglochart College in Edinburgh to prepare for becoming a teacher, at least until my long-awaited visa came through. This college was run by the Sacred Heart order, thankfully giving me a sense of continuity despite the sharp break from my sheltered life in Aberdeen.

What a surprise and comfort when I arrived to find that my special Mother MacLennan was on the Craiglochart faculty. She had literally mothered me as a frightened new boarder in Queen's Cross. I rejoiced that now I had someone to whom I could always go to talk with or to seek help from in resolving my personal problems.

That hope was rapidly dashed. Mother MacLennan was very nice, kind and proper, but I immediately felt a wall between us, a kind of distancing. Our special relationship was no more. I felt terrible. The only explanations I could think of were, first, that I was now considered an adult and needed to be weaned from my semi-dependency on her, and second, that Mother MacLennan herself may have been reminded by her superiors to sever our unusually strong bond because of her vow to devote her love only to God. Whatever the cause, I was crushed.

Blackout Years

The stress and emotions I was going through apparently wiped out from my memory most of what happened to me during my next two years at Craiglochart and before I left Scotland. I can only reconstruct a few unrelated fragments of people, events and activities.

Irene Bell befriended me. She was an *anciene élève*, as former Sacred Heart alumnae were known, and a friend of the nuns at Craiglochart. She was old enough to be my mother but invited me for teas at her apartment. I became fascinated with her collection of Hogarth prints, his cynical cartoon-like portraits of crooked judges, quack doctors and so forth.

College rules were strict—restrictions on leaving the building, specific lights-out time, and so forth. This comes to mind because a more advanced student who befriended me seemed immune from these rules. Her name was Muriel. She came from Malta and was remarkably independent. I watched with wonder as she came and went as she pleased.

Another student, Margaret Boursney, once invited me to go on the bus with her to her home. She came from a mining family. I was appalled at the grinding poverty that family endured such as I had never experienced before.

Judging from the record I kept of my grades, I must have done quite well with my studies. What I recall more clearly is the swimming pool in our building. It dated from World War I when the college was converted to a rehab hospital for wounded veterans, especially those who had suffered from poison gas. I had a passion for swimming so the pool meant a great deal to me.

Some local scenes impressed me. Our college was at the foot of an odd hill, shaped somewhat like a throne and known as Arthur's Seat. Edinburgh's main avenue, Princes Street, had buildings only along one side and an extensive park full of flowers on the other side.

If matters of consequence to me occurred during my two years in Craiglochart, they are lost in the mists of time. For example, from the police records of all my travels in Britain, which I kept, it appears that I was in Bognor Regis on the south coast of England. Put a gun to my head and I still can't say why I went there or picture anything about the place.

Finally, after ten years of waiting, my U.S. visa finally did come through and I could embark—not a happy term for a non-sailor!—on a ship across the Atlantic and onto the next phase of my life.

PART III: America

Unraveling the Conspiracy of Silence

This third part of my story is dedicated to the memory of my Aunt Mia Treuer and my Uncle Fritz—my mother's sister and brother-in-law. Their efforts to rescue my parents were truly heroic, raising funds when they were almost penniless, writing to every possible saving organization, buying tickets, all to no avail. Unable to save my mother and father, they made a home for me in America.

My Aunt Mia and Uncle Fritz

America at Last

"One small step for man, a giant leap for mankind," said Neil Armstrong in 1969 as he stepped on the moon. Twenty years earlier, for me, in July 1949, as I set foot on the pier in New York harbor, it was a giant leap into the real world.   For the first time in my life I had to face Reality and deal with it.

My Aunt Mia Treuer was there to greet me as I got off the S.S. America. My aunt was no fashionista, but even she must have been astounded as I emerged from the ship in a homemade dress and black wool stockings.   Having lived in Scotland for ten years, I couldn't believe the waves of hot air that smacked me in the face as I ran to embrace my mother's sister.   Family at last!

It was noon and Aunt Mia took me to a restaurant for lunch. I was totally unfamiliar with American money. Not having any nor wishing to have my aunt pay for something expensive, I quickly ordered a salad. Imagine my surprise and distress when the chef salad I had ordered arrived—an enormous mountain of greens, hard boiled eggs, ham and much more.   I was embarrassed and forced myself to eat it all.

Next my aunt took me to Macy's to buy two summer dresses. What a joy to put on something cool, comfortable and pretty. Off came the wool stockings.

I was starting to feel Americanized. This was only a beginning. I had a lot to learn.

As we walked in the heart of New York City suffocating hot air came out of grates in the sidewalk. I wondered: why would Americans heat city streets in the summer? Of course, I didn't know until later about vents from the subway below.

After a week in the Catskills that my aunt arranged so we could get to know each other better, it was time to go home. I eagerly looked forward to meeting Uncle Fritz again and seeing my new home in Yellow Springs, Ohio.

Steep Learning Curve

Flimsy Houses

First impressions of Yellow Springs were as bizarre as my first impressions of Scotland where men in skirts had astounded me.

Houses were made of wood. They looked alarmingly flimsy compared to the homes I was used to seeing in Aberdeen and Edinburgh, all made of granite and looking so solid. I imagined all of these wooden houses blowing away in a storm.

After greeting my uncle, I was taken upstairs to my bedroom. It had a window. Beside the bed, there was a large desk. I had arrived. I had a home.

Poor Aunt Mia and Uncle Fritz. Although strenuously anti-religious, they were very proud to be Jews. What a shock I must have given them when one of the first things I did was to hang my crucifix over the bed.

And poor me. In a sense I was looking for my mother and Aunt Mia was not at all like my mother. Uncle Fritz, nearly deaf, learned to read and write English beautifully, but speech and communications were difficult for him. He ran a bookstore back in Vienna but in Yellow Springs he could only handle menial work. So Mia wore the pants in the family. After escaping to Ohio with no funds, she not only got an accounting job but baked mountains of Viennese goodies that her son Bob peddled to college students.

Flimsy Clothing

My aunt proudly showed me around the town and then we visited Antioch College only a few blocks from her house.

As I toured the campus and dormitories, I realized immediately that I would not fit into the lifestyle I witnessed there. Young men were walking around without shirts. I was appalled to see young women with a lot of anatomy on view and wearing what struck me as shockingly short shorts. To top it off, I could not believe that bathroom doors in the dorms had no locks.

Aunt Mia had hoped I would continue my studies here in Yellow Springs. Much as I hated to disappoint her, I knew Antioch was not the place for anyone like me who had become accustomed to life in an Aberdeen convent boarding school or in an Edinburgh college run by a strict religious order.

Being the devout Catholic that I still was at the time, I introduced myself to the local priest and told him of my dilemma. He was understanding and with great kindness made arrangements for me to go to the University of Dayton, a Catholic institution about forty minutes away. He even saw to it that I got a generous scholarship which would take care of finances.

My aunt was disappointed but allowed me my freedom.

What's a Fifth Avenue?

At first I rode back and forth with Yellow Spring residents who worked in Dayton, but soon found a place that rented me a room not far from campus.

Once enrolled at UD, I was asked to spend several hours a day helping out at the little college store that sold cigarettes and candy to help pay for my tuition. Not only was I unfamiliar with the names of American candies or cigarettes, I hadn't yet learned the difference between American coins—quarters, nickels and dimes.

Students on the run to their next classes would call out to me, "Fifth Avenue," and I would have to ask whether that was a cigarette or candy and they looked at me as if I were from outer space. The same with Pall Mall and Lucky Strike. Then I would struggle to make change.

The unlucky Marianist brother in charge of the store, and whose helper I was supposed to be, had his hands full working the cash register and teaching me what was what at the same time. Eventually, nevertheless, my mentor and I bonded over our mutual love of Shakespeare and literature in general.

The two years I needed to earn my B.S. passed quickly.   I began what was to be a rather short career.

Talking on the Job

Meanwhile, even before my college classes began, I was settling in at Yellow Springs. Aunt Mia suggested it would be a good idea for me to earn some money. She arranged for me to work the night shift at Vernay Laboratory, a local firm at which, by rare diligence and usefulness to the company, she had risen to become comptroller.

I was assigned to work on a stamp press that made rubber rings or gaskets for re-frigerators, automobiles and so forth. I sat in a room with maybe twenty other women at the machines.

My job was pressing a button that made the rings fall from the machine, pushing out their centers, and placing the rings in a dish. Boring, boring, boring!

I decided that interesting conversation might make the time go faster. I tried val-iantly but got nowhere. None of the other workers responded, so finally I gave up.

At the end of the shift we all took our dishes up to a weighing station. There we also collected our pay—which depended on the number of rings we collected. My dish was by far the worst, weighing the least. Aha!

I suddenly realized there was no time for conversation, day-dreaming or whatever else that had slowed me down.

I wasn't fired but I was so glad the job ended after a short time. Then I could leave the deadly repetitive factory work and head to university and get back to earning my teaching degree.

Studying on the Job

My next job was another disaster. In between classes, I applied and got a job as sales clerk at Donnenfeld's, a fine dress shop in the heart of downtown Dayton. I was assigned to the third floor. As customers exited the elevator, clerks would rush to offer them help in finding something to buy. I held back because I knew these regular clerks worked on commission, not on a small salary like me, and I didn't want to take business away from them.

Business was slow and I had mighty little to do except stand back and watch. It dawned on me that this gave me time to read my homework assignments. When Mr. Donnenfeld spotted me standing against a back wall with a book, he asked what I was doing. I told him proudly that I was studying for my college courses. Far from being impressed at the way I was making use of my idle time, as I had expected, he fired me.

Did I have a lot to learn or what?

Teacher or Learner?

When I graduated from the University of Dayton, I applied for and was accepted as an elementary school teacher in the Dayton public school system. I was independent at last, living with a wonderful friend in a pleasant apartment. My roommate Dorothy and I took to each other as ducks to water and are friends to this day.

Idealistic or just naïve, I requested an assignment to teach difficult children. With alacrity they invited me to teach first and second grades in one of the poorest neigbborhoods in the city. My first large class was filled with kids just barely above the special-ed ability level.

As it turned out, in many ways it was my students who did the teaching. Those six-year-old first-graders were street smart and worldly wise, but they were malnourished and quite unprepared to learn anything. Their attention span was short and their eyes wandered to see what was happening on the playground. As usual, stray dogs were running around and some of them were mounting each other. With a wicked grin, one little urchin asked, "Miss, what are the dogs doing?" I felt myself blush but, keeping my composure, replied, "They're practicing to be circus dogs."

On another day one of my children brought me an exquisite bouquet. "Where did you get those flowers, Charles?" I asked. With a sweet smile came his reply, "At the cemetery."

I asked other teachers why the eyes of some of my students seemed to be dancing. It was probably due to syphilis, they told me. It soon became clear to me that many of my pupils came from homes where there were no books, magazines or even newspapers. One boy was so slow that I considered it a great victory when he learned to count to ten.

After school ended one year, I was finishing some paperwork at my desk when a woman came storming in, raving like a banshee and asking why I failed her daughter. I tried to calm her down by asking her daughter's name. As soon as she told me, I asked her, "Why didn't you call or come to see me when I sent notes home saying you and I needed to discuss why your child was not progressing?"

"Well," she screamed at me, "how would you expect her to learn when everyone else in the class was black?"

I couldn't believe this. Yet, I had a list of pupils in front of me and, as I read down I mentally pictured each face and, sure enough, all except her daughter were black. Not that that excused poor work. But it made me realize that, not having known any blacks in Austria or Scotland, I had come to America apparently completely color blind, assigning no more attention to a person's skin color than to his or her height or eye color.

From that time on I could not help noticing people's color. I became just like other race-conscious Americans.

From Dream World to Reality

I can't recall how it gradually seeped into my mind that my parents had probably perished. Even though I had no real news, it was just too long for them not to have contacted me.

Nor can I remember when I came to know for certain that my family was Jewish, and that the vicious Nazi campaign against Jews explained a large part of the course my life had taken.

Nor can I recall how my Catholicism gradually waned. I do know that I seriously tried to seek out Catholic companions in America. Curiously, friends that I was most comfortable with often turned out to be Jewish.

I do not blame myself for living in a dream world for the first two decades of my life. My parents' letters to me in Scotland were almost always reassuring, advising me not to worry and to pray that everything would turn out well. I now possess correspondence between the adult family members during those years. Again and again my relatives reminded each other not to tell me bad news.

Parents' Last Days in Vienna

"My dear darling Erika," began a long letter in difficult-to-read German from Aunt Olga Kraft, a Catholic relative in Vienna. World War II was over so correspondence between Austria and Britain was again possible. She wrote to me in Aberdeen in October 1946. She did not address me as a child, breaking the old conspiracy of silence. She gave me perhaps the first inkling that I might be Jewish. Here, considerably condensed, is what she wrote:

After you left [on the Kindertransport] **your parents were terribly distressed. They were moved to Rudolfstrasse** [a Jewish ghetto]. **As an old friend, I stood by them. It became more and more difficult for**

Jews. Twice a week your friend Helmut [Olga's son] brought a knapsack of food from our vegetable garden and treats from Hotel Bristol where Lisl [her daughter] worked. He went late in the evening so he wouldn't be seen. Wonderful Aunt Ella and Gretl Gebauer sacrificed a great deal too. Praise be to Karl Novak, head gardener from Hohenau, who brought me all sorts of things which I secretly got to your parents.

In fall 1941 began the unhappy transports to Poland. We tried every means to permit your parents to locate outside Vienna, to no avail despite his World War I injuries and medals. They were given only two days notice. Mimi Pollock and I spent both days and nights getting household things moved. Your mother wanted me to save her fur coat but we insisted she take it plus warm clothes and blankets to fend off the cold in Poland. Your parents sewed money into clothes—shilling notes—to use there. They had a little money because for weeks we had been selling off their furniture.

On the last day Novak brought a roast chicken with all the fixings for the trip. We had a difficult farewell. Papi and Mutti talked touchingly about their love for you, dear Erika, wishing you to be happy and content. They were so courageous, consoling and comforting us. From Lodz they wrote that two other couples who worked with them in a lace factory were on the same train.

Every week Aunt Gretl, Aunt Ella and I each sent them 20 shillings from the money they had left with us. After a short while they asked that we send no more. Then I learned that only Jews were permitted to send money to Jews. Others could be jailed, lose their jobs or their pensions if the Gestapo found out. The Pollocks underwent four searches from them.

We packed what was left of your folks' belongings in six trunks and took them to Gretl Gebauer. I had the rest of their money, 1500 shillings. Another 4000 was in a savings account. Your father was forced to tear up all records concerning that account and declare that he willingly gave up the funds. Now Herr Girtler, director of that bank, tells me we should do nothing about confiscated "Arianized" assets until the government decides how to handle such matters.

Papa gave his valuable solitaire diamond ring to a friend to pass on to his cousin Victor Goldschmidt, a college professor in Norway, whom I once met at your parents' house.

Suddenly Uncle Karl Gebauer, who was not Jewish, fell ill. Aunt Gretl who was Jewish feared his death would leave her at the mercy of the Nazis. Thus she asked me to take Papa's gold watch and trunks filled with china, porcelain, linen, clothes and the rest. Everything could be lost so I put them in storage with your nice dining furniture that I had previously bought. That storage place was bombed twice and almost everything was destroyed—except those six trunks and the dining furniture!

Then came the occupation by the SS and everything went topsy-turvy and was wrecked. Street gangs broke the locks on the trunks and plundered the dresses and linen, leaving one silk undergarment and one tuxedo shirt. I located the trunks and found an SS uniform and Nazi books left on them. Plates, platters and glasses were in pieces but underneath were beautiful crystal which had been particularly well packed. They are in our cellar until we can send them to you.

When Karl was ill their whole block and their entire apartment burned down, so everything of your family's would have been lost. Uncle Karl recovered so Gretl was saved. The Meitlinger's house was totally destroyed. Aunt Ella Popper's place in the Nikolaigasse was so heavily bombed, it's hard to believe anybody lives there—but she does and it's her seventieth birthday. She is head of the apartment, very smart, very capable and healthy too. [My husband and I visited Aunt Ella in 1956, still living in the same place, and some apartments still had no walls, exposed to the air.]

About our family. Uncle Franz is manager of a sanitarium. Helmut fortunately was not wounded in the war; he studied English and economics and last week gave a well-received lecture to the League of

Nations. Lisl studied home economics, works at Hotel Bristol and soon will be marrying a nice businessman. We all four suffered enough during the Hitler years.

Now I embrace you. Greetings to Fritz and Mia, and to Bobby, his wife and baby. Does Mia remember what good friends we were in our youth? God bless you and be happy in America.

Aunt Olga thought when she wrote this that I was on my way to America. It took another three years before that happened. At that time she and Uncle Franz did send me the remnants of my parents' possessions.

Poignant Letters

What was going through my parents' minds when we suddenly left Hohenau and when they let me think this was simply a nice change to move in with my grandmother in Vienna? Nothing answers this question better than the revealing letters my father composed to send to people in the sugar factor he had managed and from which he had just been expelled.

August 1938

TO THE EMPLOYEES OF THE HOHENAU SUGAR FACTORY

Dear Fellow Employees:

Now, after a thirty-year long association in this establishment, and only several years before my pension becomes available, through no fault of mine fate has forced me to give up my life's work and my country and I go with my family toward a dark future.

In this moment I feel moved to say farewell to you all and especially those with whom I have worked side by side for so many years. How much I would like to shake each one of you by the hand, but that is not possible, because that would be beyond my strength to endure. Therefore I say farewell in this manner and thank you all for your faithful association and discipline.

Continue to be good comrades and continue to live together in peace and camaraderie and sometimes remember me with friendly thoughts.

(Signed) Dr. Schulhof

<u>August 1938</u>

TO THE HONORABLE MANAGEMENT OF THE HOHENAU SUGAR FACTORY

In this moment of time through undeserved bad luck, my life's work has been rendered useless, as well as robbing me of my homeland. Many bitter words force themselves from my lips against those colleagues whose participation resulted in this for my family and me. But I won't speak out. Rather I will try to forgive those who must take this blame on their conscience.

For all other colleagues who have been loyal through so many years and have expressed their empathy for my hard luck, I would like personally to take my leave from them but I cannot bear it. I simply wouldn't be able to do it. All of those people I thank from the bottom of my heart. May their future at least be sunny in spite of my misfortune. May you think of me kindly.

(Signed) Dr. Schulhof

"Robbing me of my homeland" jumped out at me when I found these letters. Papi already suspected his fate three years before he and Mutti were deported.

People Misunderstand

I gradually learned the horrible facts of the Nazi murder machinery that occurred while I was overprotected, first by my parents and then by the nuns. What was quite painful was the reaction of friends and acquaintances who, from my perspective, misunderstood my story.

"You couldn't not have known you were Jewish," some declared. It's possible that I missed signals along the way. But it is not pleasant to have people, with a wink and a smile, imply that I am a liar—as many people implied when Secretary of State Madeleine Albright said she had not known she was Jewish. Suggestions that I was denying my Jewish heritage are not easy to rebut, but how could I have denied what I did not know? I could not have been more proud of my background once I learned that my family of Sephardic Jews, starting back in the Iberian Peninsula, included generations of rabbis who produced long lines of accomplished achievers.

"Aren't you angry at your parents for hiding you from the evils swirling around you?" On the contrary, I marvel at their ability to give me a genuine childhood and such a strong sense of love and security that they have supported me throughout my life.

"Didn't people ever ask you about your religion?" The question reflects the difficulty of Americans, and especially Jews of Eastern European background, to comprehend the culture of assimilation that prevailed in professional and artistic circles after Austria offered full citizenship rights to Jews. Austrians of my parents' generation also told me that in the pre-Hitler era inquiring about one's religion "just wasn't done." They compared it to the typical American taboo of asking acquaintances how much money they make.

"Why didn't your parents get out?" I myself wondered about that, incorrectly assuming that in our little village of Hohenau they did not realize the dangers facing them. Only when I came into Aunt Mia's collection of her correspondence with my parents and other papers did I realize the frantic efforts by my parents and the Treuers to get visas and safe passage. At times these efforts came tantalizingly close as they got papers and even plane or ship tickets to New Zealand, the Philippines, Turkey, Norway, Portugal and China, as well as to the United States, only to be thwarted by the advance of Hitler's war machine, by bureaucratic deception and ineptness, or quirks of fate. Time after time their high hopes failed to materialize.

"Turning Catholic didn't save them, did it?" This judgment by those who didn't know my parents' motives infuriates me. Unlike me, my folks were not ignorant of their Jewish heritage. They had to be well informed of Hitler's edict that anyone with a Jewish grandparent was marked for eradication. They could have had no illusion that converting would save them, any more than my father's World War I medals would save him. They converted to save me, which it did. My anger led me to write the following poem about those who presumed that my parents "should have known better." One can decide who are the other they's I refer to.

WHO SHOULD HAVE KNOWN BETTER?

They should have known better.

But **they** tried to make peace with a tyrant.

They turned in friends and neighbors for deportation and death.

They closed their borders to those who pleaded for shelter.

They denied visas and let cries for help go unanswered.

God knows **they** should have known better.

After joining the Child Survivors of the Holocaust, it struck me that I and most of the group had put our traumas on the back burner in order to get on with our lives. Those traumas came back to haunt us, which led me to write the following.

CHAMELEON

We've blended well

For fifty years.

Why now the anger and the tears

As we move close to the abyss

Still looking for a mother's kiss?

The Lucky Ones

Many of us who survived the war years in Europe as children only started coming out of the closet, so to speak, when the Child Survivors of the Holocaust was formed some three decades after the war. Why had our "silent generation" taken so long, until we reached our fifties, to come to terms with our unique experience?

We were the lucky ones, people told us.

As children our lives often depended on our silence. Our elders reinforced this behavior even after all danger passed. Children, it was widely assumed, were too young to have been traumatized. We bought into the myth of how lucky we were and got on with our lives, suppressing emotions that did not agree with this assessment of our good luck. I was well into middle age when someone called me "the queen of denial." This made me angry because I refused to believe her, but she was right.

Sure, we were lucky that we escaped and were not gassed. But was it good fortune that many of us lost parents and relatives, lost our homes, country and native language, and lost contact with anything familiar or secure? We children who were supposedly untouched by events that fundamentally changed our lives were given few explanations and no support for emotional and physical upheavals.

Once childhood trauma became recognized as a reality, issues and memories I had packed away came flooding back. For years and years I could not speak German or even understand letters I had saved from my parents, but amazingly the language of my first decade returned. It was comforting to find that other child survivors shared my feelings. Like me, they were uncomfortable with casual departures by family and friends. We seemed excessively bothered by little setbacks. At one child survivor meeting, a successful banker, in the midst of telling his escape story, suddenly broke down, saying he realized for the first time that he was an orphan. My images of pitiful orphans came from storybooks. I didn't like being part of those stories either.

Answers Half a Century Later

For years I wrote every possible organization, in America, Austria and Israel, trying to discover why, despite the German's meticulous record keeping, nobody could tell me of my parents' last days. As recently as 1996 I received another of the periodic Red Cross letters saying they were still trying to trace what happened to my mother and father.

January 22, 1996

Mrs. Erika Rybeck
10615 Brunswick Avenue
Kensington, MD 20895

Case Number   : ISS-H-0675
Sought Person : Friedrich SCHULHOF

Dear Mrs. Rybeck;

With reference to our letter of January 30, 1995 and the above mentioned tracing inquiry, please be advised that no information has become available yet, but our tracing efforts are continuing through the International Tracing Service, Arolsen.

I am sorry that we do not have more complete news to report to you at this time. The case is remaining open and when further information becomes available, we will notify you immediately.

They simply confirmed that they were deported from Vienna on October 23, 1941 on a train headed for Lodz, Poland. There the trail ended. It was not until 2002 that, thanks to my son Rick and his wife, Ellen Czaplewski, I finally learned their fate. Over half a century after the war in Europe ended, the following is what Rick and Ellen discovered, as excerpted from a detailed account by Rick.

In summer 2002 we tacked a trip to Poland onto my business trip to Germany. Our itinerary took us from Gdansk to Skarzevy (origin of some of Ellen's family), to Krakow and nearby Auschwitz, to Tarnov (more of Ellen's family came from there), to Brno (Erika's mother's Czech birthplace), and on to Lodz.

When buying tickets, the travel agent asked why we were going to Poland. Ellen said Erika's parents had been deported from Vienna to Lodz. By coincidence, the woman agent said she had just returned from a memorial service for her family members who also had been deported to Lodz and perished there. She gave us the name of Hubert Rogozinski of the Lodz Jewish community who tracks missing relatives.

Grateful for that piece of luck, I wrote him, asking for information about my grandparents. I gave him the names of Friedrich and Gertrude Schulhof and the date we would arrive in Lodz.

We arrived by train at Lodz at 10 a.m. I was apprehensive, not knowing what we would find there. In the taxi to the address we had been given, we drove past buildings or retaining walls that contained graffiti including Stars of David. Odd.

Hubert said he had hired a driver for a day tour of Lodz with his son serving as interpreter. This sounded expensive and made me nervous. We were at the end of our trip and our money was low. I decided to buy a little time instead. "Before we go anywhere," I said, "could you tell me if you found out anything about my grandparents."

"Good news. We found that they registered upon their arrival." I was overjoyed. For years, Mom knew nothing of her parents after they were deported from Vienna. Now we could say that they arrived in Lodz. Yet joy turned to panic with a suspicion. Since many Americans come for news of lost relatives, wouldn't it be easy for my host to make up almost any story to leave us feeling grateful for the information?

Just as this thought came to me, Hubert said, "By the way, did you know that your grandparents were Catholic?" Joy returned. I never shared the news of their conversion with Hubert, so this statement was a sign that his information was indeed genuine.

"Your grandparents were registered, at 13 Lotnicza Street," he added. This address did not exist any longer. Later, not far from there, we were shown two old wooden buildings of the type they lived in. Hubert promised to do more research and send us his findings. True to his word, he faxed my grandparent's registration card. Mom recognized her father's signature. This alone made the visit worthwhile.

My father's registration in Lodz.—clearly in his handwriting

Then Hubert wrote that when the Lodz Ghetto was liquidated, my grandparents were not deported with Jews from Vienna because they chose to go with a group of Christians who were deported to Chelmno May 9, 1942, leaving at 7 a.m. and arriving that afternoon. This is the last known record of my grandparents.

According to Hubert and my own research, Chelmno was not a concentration camp but purely a death camp prior to invention of gas chambers. Prisoners were forced to disrobe before being put into the cargo hold of trucks which were sealed off. Then truck exhaust was piped in as the truck drove around until people stopped moving. Bodies of those who perished were dumped in a nearby forest.

Rick and Ellen did not tell me of their quest before they went to Poland for fear they would learn nothing and compound my sense of loss. Although the news they brought back was tragic, their careful planning, the pains they took to get the facts, and even the tragic news itself gave me comfort. No longer would I have to await letters telling me, "Proof of death is not available," or "no information has become available yet." Knowing the awful truth is a relief after spending most of my life trying to fathom how my wonderful parents could have vanished into thin air.

My 2011 Tsunami

A favorite piece of music, Verdi's Requiem, was advertised in the Washington Post. I attended, wondering why they called it "The Defiant Requiem." The Kennedy Center's enormous concert hall was packed. The National Symphony Orchestra augmented by a chorus of 300 singers gave an inspired performance. During the powerful Dies Irae the very walls seemed to tremble. When the last note was played, the audience, spellbound, walked out in perfect silence.

Why It Was Called Defiant

Between each segment of the mass, on a big screen behind the orchestra, survivors of the Czech concentration camp, Terezin (Theresienstadt in German), told their unbelievable story. During World War II the Nazis used this camp as a "model" to fool the world about their death camps. Red Cross examiners saw a cleaned-up camp, heard lectures by prisoners, attended musical performances, and saw happy children at play, unaware that these well-fed youngsters had been brought in from outside for the inspection events.

Rafael Schächter

A remarkable musician prisoner, Rafael Schächter, using an old upright and with only one copy of the score, taught by rote all the parts of the long, dramatic and difficult Verdi mass to half-starving fellow prisoners.

The Nazis didn't get it. Officers, guards and visiting commanders were amused by Jews singing a Catholic mass. The prisoners, however, were uplifted by singing to their captors what they could not speak. What they could not speak was the central message of the mass, namely, that evil would be punished while the righteous would be blessed. The singers lifted their voices to proclaim this message sixteen different times.

Reviving the Terezin Marvel

Murry Sidlin, conductor of the Defiant Requiem, had learned of this story, tracked down survivors and reproduced the concentration camp performance several times, including at Terezin itself. Two friends of mine in the chorus at Terezin found it so emotional they said it was all they could do to keep singing. Easily understandable. After hearing the Kennedy Center performance, I was sure I would never again have such a powerful and moving experience. I was wrong.

The Story Goes On

As soon as I got home I called cousin Bob to tell him of this amazing performance. He responded with the surprising news that Conductor Murry Sidlin whom we had just heard would re-create the Defiant Requiem in Bemidji, his Minnesota home town. Equally surprising and even more heartwarming, Bob had arranged for the program to be dedicated to the memory of my parents, other relatives of Bob's and mine, and to all others who had perished in the Holocaust.

How was this possible? Beverly Everett, conductor of the Bemidji Symphony, was a former student of Sidlin's. She pleaded with him to bring this program to her small community. When Sidlin agreed, Beverly told Bob who is a friend and strong supporter of the symphony. Together they worked out the dedication.

Keeping Expectations in Check

After the stirring performance in Washington, I was prepared for a letdown. The Bemidji high school, after all, was not the Kennedy Center. The choir and orchestra members were locals and from nearby Minnesota communities.

On the morning of the event, thirty members of our families gathered in a motel meeting room. Someone spotted Conductor Sidlin in the lobby and invited him to join us. He immediately gravitated to photos of my parents and others we had set up in the room. Of special interest to Sidlin were pictures of our Czech relatives, Aunt Ellie and Uncle Bertie Epstein and their son Hans, all of whom died at Terezin.

We listened spellbound as Sidlin related how he accidentally came across a book noting that Terezin prisoners had sung the Verdi Requiem. This so intrigued him that he spent years of detective work, finding Terezin survivors to piece their stories together, and then creating a documentary to accompany the music.

Only in America

An unlikely event in an unlikely setting: Near the front of the packed audience in the Bemidji high school auditorium was a solid row of Rybecks and Treuers sitting together to honor the memory of family members who had perished. Half of our group was Jewish and the other half Native Americans since Bob had an Ojibwe wife. Here was a coming together of two families of two persecuted peoples condemned to the ash heaps of history—still living, loving, and affirming life and liberty—honoring those who did not live to see this remarkable day!

A Fitting Memorial

Somewhere in a Polish forest lie the remains of my mother and father. They were murdered by the Nazis at Chelmno as part of Germany's "final solution." No grave, tombstone or acknowledgement offers proof that they had existed—a truth I lived with for too long.

For the first time since their horrible deaths in 1942, hidden in mystery until 2002, I finally felt free to grieve for them as their lives were validated during a most moving

Conductor Sidlin

performance of the Defiant Requiem. It was Sunday, May 1, 2011 in Bemidji, Minnesota.

A haunting Jewish melody played by solo violin introduced this unique interplay of Jewish and Christian musical expressions. Then Verdi's passionate mass held the audience enthralled. Remarkably, the local orchestra and choir matched the Kennedy Center performance for virtuosity and emotional content. Two of the four professional vocal soloists were the ones I had heard in Washington. The atmosphere seemed even more intense in this more intimate setting.

The continuous prayer, "Requiem aeternam," was sung with fervor and emotion: "Eternal rest give unto them O Lord and let perpetual light shine upon them." The caressing notes and the healing words made for a calm start to the thunderous calls for justice which soon followed. After the final plea for eternal rest, the musicians silently left the stage one by one as the solo violinist played Oseh shalom, a well-known prayer of peace from the Jewish liturgy. Again the audience filed out in utter silence.

What an honor it was for my parents to be remembered at long last in such a fitting fashion.

Discovering Ancestors

Among my parents' belongings that were saved for me was a Stammbaum, a precious family tree of Porges und Porges von Portheim. My mother and father are both listed in different branches of the huge family. A note indicates that the first named person, Rabbi Jechiel Micht, lived in the time of the Inquisition, from about 1500 to 1550.

The earliest precisely dated names start in the 1600s—seven rabbis all named Spiro. I've been told that such old records are almost nonexistent except for rabbis. Presumably having come from Portugal, Rabbi Wolf Spiro settled in Prague. Rabbi Simon Spiro never stayed put, moving from Frankfurt to Lemberg, Lublin, Litthauen, Krakau and Vienna. One of the rabbi's sons married into the Porges family.

Handwritten notices of more recent births, deaths and weddings add to the interest of this document, which is accompanied by a beautiful tooled leather-bound volume of old photographs.

An Emperor's Modified Offer

How could a Jewish family, I wondered, end up with such a noble title as von Portheim? Detective work by nephew Ted Rybeck unearthed the story in 2010 when he took his wife Ellen and their daughters to Prague, Brno, Vienna and Hohenau.

Ted learned that Moses Porges and Leopold Juda Porges, two poor brothers, paid attention to progressive manufacturing processes in one of their journeys. To run a calico or cotton printing plant in the Prague outskirts, they introduced the city's first steam engine around 1808. It is recorded that Emperor Ferdinand I, whose Austrian empire then included Prague, was promoting modernization and, saw the Porges' plant. He was so impressed with this application of steam power that, like in a fairy tale, he offered the brothers whatever they wished.

This was a time when most Jews, confined to live in ghettos, faced severe restrictions. The Porges brothers promptly expressed their wish: EQUALITY FOR THE

JEWS.

The emperor, taken aback, said they had asked too much. However, as an alternative, on June 5, 1841, he bestowed full citizen rights to the brothers and their descendents plus the hereditary nobility title of Edle von Portheim. Portheim signified "home of the port" based on the Porges family's origins in Porto, Portugal. Nearly unheard of in those days were Jews enjoying the status of nobility.

Ted figured out that Leopold Porges (1784-1869) was my great, great, great grandfather.

Hub of Culture

The Porges brothers created a handsome villa or mansion called Portheimka with lovely gardens. They loved music and supported artists. Moses' son Joseph von Portheim continued the musical tradition and hosted lectures there. He played the cello and inaugurated chamber music concerts. Antonin Dvorak, a member of the group, played in Portheimka every other Sunday. This famous composer dedicated one of his pieces to Joseph.

Portheimka Villa in Prague suburb

The last family member to own the villa, Karel von Portheim, committed suicide when the Nazis invaded Czechoslovakia. The public took the villa over and it exists now as an art gallery, as Ted could attest after his visit there.

Honoring My Relatives

It is hard to express how touched I was to learn that, after leaving Prague, Ted, Ellen, and their daughters, Mia and Emma, went to Terezin and then to Brno out of respect for me. At Terezin they all said a prayer for the Epsteins—Aunt Elly, Uncle Bertie and cousin Hansi who died there. Only Hansi's sister, my cousin Nelly, survived in that family. She escaped by hiking all across Europe until she reached what is now Israel where she lived to an old age.

In Brno, where my mother and her two sisters were born, Ted and family paid respects to my Grandparents Weil who died long before I was born. My grandfather, Ted learned, was so highly respected in this capital city of Moravia that the emperor sent a member of the Imperial Guard to accompany the casket during his funeral procession. Ted's family actually retraced that procession from the site of the Great Synagogue of Brno—which was burned and destroyed by the Nazis—to the cemetery. They cleaned off the moss-covered headstone of my grandparents and read the following inscription, as translated into English:

NELLY WEIL, born May 20, 1871, died September 19, 1910, the best wife and mother.

KARL WEIL, Brno Chief of Public Works, born July 3, 1862, died January 5, 1912, the best father, the most loving son, what more words need one say?

:

Full Circle

As if Ted had not done enough, he went back to the Austrian village of Hohenau on the River March, on the Czech border, where I had experienced the first phase of my life. He visited with Hilda Drabek, my first grade teacher, still sharp in her late nineties, and her daughter Maria Tandinger, a teacher of math, physics and art.

Contrary to my childhood sense that Hohenau was a tiny village with nothing but a sugar factory, Ted learned that it was an important European crossroads with a proud history going back hundreds of years. I was astounded to hear him say there is an interesting museum about the city and even more astounded that he saw a Jewish cemetery that he was told had served an ancient Jewish community. Until then, I had always assumed there were few if any Jews in my home town.

All this was another reminder of the degree to which I was cut off from reality during my nine "magic kingdom years" in Hohenau.

Postscript—The Rest of My Life

I have told as best I can remember many of the things that shaped my life in Austria, Scotland and my early years in America. What happened next? I summarize briefly the longest phase of my life.

In 1954 I became an American citizen and married Walter Rybeck, an editorial writer on the Dayton Daily News.

I continued teaching. It struck me as scandalous that supplies and services, which were meager or nonexistent in my earlier school in a slum, were abundant and first-rate when I transferred to a school in a more upscale neighborhood. We joined the Jewish reform temple and enjoyed folk dancing, bird watching, classical music and helped start a new nature museum. Walt's family in Wheeling, West Virginia, and I became enmeshed in a mutual love affair. Two sons, Rick and Alex, came along in rapid succession. On

weekends we shared meals with Aunt Mia and Uncle Fritz at our home or theirs in Yellow Springs.

When Walt was named Washington bureau chief for Cox Newspapers, we moved to Kensington, Maryland in 1961. We developed new sets of close friends and partook of the rich cultural life of the capital area.

As our boys grew, I participated in a wide range of volunteer activities, starting with being a den mother for Cub Scouts. I led a group that helped wives of junior diplomats learn English and American customs.

I took courses in acupressure and was able, much to my own surprise at first, to give pain relief to a number of clients during my four years of practice. My friend from Scotland, Chris Tabor Garber, and I then did catering for several years. We made no money but had a great time and pleased our customers who got delicious dinners at ridiculously low prices.

I did a stint at a crisis center, advising call-ins who faced various forms of peril. It was another opportunity to learn about real life—on the seamier side.

Our garden, full of azaleas and all kinds of shade-loving flowers, was a great pleasure. On the deck I designed we could watch the hummingbirds, take many of our meals and marvel at the gothic arches formed by the branches of the tall oaks in and around our property.

When the boys were old enough to enjoy traveling, we spent memorable vacations with them in Austria and Scotland, of course, and also in Ireland, England, France, Yugoslavia, Switzerland, Spain, Andorra and Italy as well as in Canada and the United States.

On a happy note, I became closer to Aunt Mia as she aged. I reveled in the fact that my cousin Bob, Mia's only child, had a huge family of children, grandchildren and even great grandchildren. I dearly loved Walt's father until he died at age 70, and my relationship with his mother could not have been closer. She was a real mother to me until she died at 99. Arthur, Walt's brother, and his large family also brought me much joy.

In my mid-70s I watched a number of our older friends find it difficult to cope with managing their homes. To avoid that, we moved into Riderwood Village, a retirement community not far from our Maryland home and still in the Washington, DC, area. It was among my best decisions. A new circle of wonderful caring friends makes our retirement years a delight. The major negative part, since most of us who live here are of "that age," is that we frequently lose dear companions.

AGING

Old age comes on kitten paws
Then all at once
with tiger claws
that rip your flesh
and rake your soul
and hold you fast
as windows open
to your past
and wrestle with you
for control.

—Erika Schulhof Rybeck

Life Works on a Compensating Balance

This was the title given to our class for an essay while I was still in high school. I can't remember what I wrote, but I had no idea what the topic meant. From time to time throughout my life I've wondered about it.

In America I reinvented myself for the third time. Often I was in denial that I was an orphan, that I had a strange childhood, that for years I had had no home, that I had missed adolescence, that most of my family were gone and that I had unfinished grieving to do. Basically, I was alone in the world. I would never have the satisfaction of my parents being proud of me for overcoming difficulties. Meanwhile I hardly noticed, as I worked through these traumas, that my life's balance had shifted significantly. Life has been good. I can acknowledge the compensating balance my life has attained, thanks to my wonderful husband and two sons and the experiences we shared. My long-ago class assignment is finally completed and understood.

I conclude by saying how proud I am of my sons. Rick is an economist, city planner and consultant, married to Ellen, a successful realtor with many talents. Alex is a music director, arranger, composer and pianist. While I am pleased with their considerable professional achievements, what pleases me most is that they are good human beings, doing their bit to make the world a better place.

Acknowledgements

I wrote this account of some of my experiences simply to satisfy my need to sift through matters that had confused me, and for the family. Dorothy Raphael, one of my longest and dearest friends, got me to change directions when she *demanded* that I put my story in book form as my legacy and as a memorial to my parents. Thank you, Dorothy!

Before my parents were transported from Vienna to Poland, they gave various possessions to Aunt Olga and Uncle Franz Kraft, distant Catholic members of our family, to stash away until what they hoped would be their return to Austria. When my parents were presumed dead, and after I went to America, the Krafts sent me silverware, documents and photos of my early years, a sampling of which are in this book. For storing and saving them: thanks, Mutti and Papi and the Krafts.

Many photos were in poor shape due to age, transport and unprofessional care. I am indebted to Robert Boger for generously giving his time and his expertise in making them as clear as possible. Dear friend Won Yin worked her magic to bring back to life a tiny thumbnail photo of my parents in front of the garden fence. Special friend Jessie Heron who once lived in Ellon found for me pictures of The Chestnuts and Ellon Castle where I had stayed.

Unaccustomed as I am with publishing, Eileen McIntire of Columbia, Maryland, came to my rescue. I am grateful to her for bringing my memoir into print.

For their unexpected research and findings into what happened to my parents, half a century after their death, I am deeply grateful to my son Rick and his wife Ellen. I also thank Alex, my other son, both for valuable suggestions for this story and for composing a moving tribute to my parents, *Adagietto*, which always brings tears to my eyes.

My husband Walter put the manuscript on the computer, helped with the sequence of my story, and pushed me when I needed pushing. He knows how much I appreciate him. As the song from *The Most Happy Fella* goes, "My heart is so full of you...there is no room for anything more."

CPSIA information can be obtained at www.ICGtesting.com
Printed in the USA
BVOW10s0041191214

380080BV00009B/475/P